Writing Handbooks

Writing
Romantic
Fiction

Writing Handbooks

Writing Romantic Fiction

Daphne Clair
and Robyn Donald

A & C Black • London

First published 1999
A & C Black (Publishers) Limited
35 Bedford Row, London WC1R 4JH

© 1999 Daphne Clair and Robyn Donald

ISBN 0–7136–4887–2

A CIP catalogue record for this book
is available from the British Library.

Typeset in 10½ on 12 pt Sabon
Printed and bound in Great Britain by
Creative Print and Design (Wales), Ebbw Vale

Contents

To Frances Whitehead and Lesley Wainger – editors of discernment and distinction who know their three R's — readers, 'riters and romance.

Dear Writer: Introduction

Writing a romance is much harder than it looks. In all the world only about two thousand people are successful, multi-published romance writers. Our aim in this book is to make your path to publication a little less rugged.

Each of us had our first romance released by Mills & Boon in 1977. Between us we have had over a hundred romantic novels published. This book is the result of all that experience.

Our definition of a romance is: a story in which the plot is driven by a sexually based emotional relationship between two people. And for most readers there has to be a happy ending – or at least the strong implication of future happiness.

Tales of love are one of the oldest forms of popular literature because they deal with important things – love, birth, relationships, families, and sometimes death. Thus they appeal to a wide readership; Japanese and Hungarian, Korean and Brazilian, Turkish and African women enjoy them as much as do women in English-speaking countries.

Romantic novels account for half the mass-market paperback book sales in the English language. And who reads all these books? Women. Men read adventure fantasies about conquering the world and taming the wilds; women read adventure fantasies about taming men and conquering their hearts.

Readership surveys conducted in Britain in 1974 by Dr Peter Mann, Reader in Sociology at Sheffield University, and in the USA by Dr Carol Thurston (1987), show that women who read romances follow the normal curve of distribution. So among romance readers there are exactly the same proportion of 17-year-old scholarship students, 27-year-old jet pilots, 37-year-old beekeepers, 47-year-old nurses and 57-year-old barristers as there are among women in general.

In the 1990s in North America 50 million women are romance readers, and 70 per cent of these women have attended or graduated from college. Readership surveys show that romance readers are better educated than the average woman.

Women who read romantic fiction read widely in other forms of fiction and nonfiction. They tend not to watch much television, and when they do it's usually news, documentaries and films. They fit the statistical norms for working outside the home.

In order to write successfully for these women you must respect both their choice of reading material and their intelligence.

Don't try to write romances if you've never read one; you need to immerse yourself in them so you can recognise the clichés to avoid and find out whether your heart yearns to write a long family saga of over a hundred thousand words or a short category romance as published by Harlequin, Silhouette and Mills & Boon. Write the books you'd love to read.

And don't believe anyone who suggests there is only one way to write. We will give you various methods that we and other writers use, but ultimately you must choose what works for you.

All advice on how to write – including ours – should be taken with a grain of salt, and there is no rule which cannot be broken in the interests of a better story.

This book is based on notes for courses we run in New Zealand, and workshops we have conducted at conferences in New Zealand, Australia and America. These notes are continually modified and updated as markets change and as we learn more about what aspiring writers need to help them towards successful publication. When you have read the book, you will need to keep your own knowledge updated by reading new romances as they appear. See also the advice in the chapter Occupation – Writer, p. 92. It is also useful to subscribe to romance and readers' magazines and join writing groups.

We have labelled the chapters by subject, but this is an artificial division – as in juggling, all the balls have to be deployed at the same time, so sometimes we've repeated certain things in different sections. We suggest you read the whole book through, absorb the advice so that it percolates through your unconscious, then go back and re-read relevant sections when you need them.

Good luck and good writing.

1. What It's All About

Romance writers enjoy re-creating for their readers that wonderful feeling of being in love, with its uncertainties and excitement, its pain and its pleasure.

Writing romance is as difficult and demanding as any other form of writing. It is very focused, leaving little room for self-indulgent fine writing, irrelevant subplots, soap-boxing, or side-issues of importance only to the writer.

Perhaps more than in any other genre, the ending is almost always predicated in the beginning. Some readers habitually flip first to the final page to reassure themselves that the author has not cheated them of the expected happy ending. Others will tolerate a less predictable outcome, but for many (including editors) it is as much a given of the romance genre as is the revelation of whodunnit at the end of a murder mystery.

Reader expectation must be met. At the same time the writer must feed the reader's desire to be delighted and satisfied by the eventual resolution of a seemingly insurmountable problem. The romance writer aims to keep the reader interested and excited about what will happen next, even though that reader knows what will happen in the end. It takes considerable skill to write in a fresh, unforgettable way a story that has been told over and over since the beginning of time; to keep the reader in suspense not about *who* or *what* but about *how* and *why*.

Good romance writers are also regular readers who love the genre. It is unprofessional and insulting to your readers to despise what you're doing, and you are not likely to be good at writing something you dislike. Romance writers may not garner much respect in literary and academic circles, but you need to respect yourself and your work – and your readers, who are intelligent, widely read and observant.

These readers want to be entertained, and want to see your heroine win the hero she deserves. They won't be entertained if your research is sloppy, if your writing is difficult to read, if they can't like your hero or heroine, or if your manuscript has great, yawning plot holes.

If you are a new writer, inexperienced in any genre, you may find it useful to start by reading the Appendix at the end of the book, which includes general techniques for writing fiction, slanted towards romance but applicable to other genres.

Preparation

Having studied basic fiction techniques, decide what kind of book you want to write. A short category romance of about 55,000 words? A longer category book, up to 75,000 or 85,000 words? A 100,000-word single title romance for a mainstream publisher?

Would you rather write historicals? Gothics? Romantic suspense? Blockbusting family sagas with a central romance or serial romances? Or perhaps not even a romance at all.

The hero and heroine are the focus of the straightforward romance and need to feature strongly on almost every page. Filter everything through their eyes, and keep them centre stage. For the purposes of this book we've named our hero and heroine Slade and Melinda (except for quotes from published books) – they've had a very chequered lovelife, as you will see.

Don't assume the first manuscript you write will be snapped up by an eager publisher. It can happen, but it's unusual. Romances are difficult to write well because they are so tightly focused – in the same way that a short story, poem or children's picture book can be more difficult to get right than a mainstream novel.

In discussing the central motivation and underlying cause of problems between your hero and heroine we have coined the phrase 'source of tension', rather than using 'conflict' which has been called the basis of all fiction. We found 'conflict' gave first-time writers the idea that their hero and heroine had to snap and snarl at each other all through the book, which is not so. The term 'source of tension' gets closer to the crux of the book – whatever it is that is keeping these two from falling in love instantly, and making a lifelong commitment to the other person at the end of Chapter One.

The source of tension is based around the characters' personalities, past, fears and responsibilities, and your plot will be built on it. This is discussed more deeply later in the book.

Planning

There is no correct way to write a book, no single right way to produce a manuscript. There are writers who have time charts and biographies of their characters and lists of necessary information and know each plot step before they start. And there are those who begin with a name, a picture, a vague idea or an opening scene – sometimes with nothing at all but a single word on the screen – and 'wing it' from there.

Both of us tend to be wingers rather than planners, although Robyn's first draft is a much sketchier, more incomplete affair than Daphne's. But there are great advantages in planning.

You may start with your characters and build your plot from there; or you may prefer to start with a plot and create characters that will fit that plot. Or a combination of both.

Choose the way that suits you best – beware of 'how-to' books that promote only that particular writer's methods.

We know successful writers who:

♥ Scribble scene or plot point ideas on cards and shuffle them about until a logical plot sequence appears.

♥ Write disconnected scenes and join them together with narrative bridges later.

♥ Think about a story for months until it is all in their head, then write it down in two weeks or less.

♥ Write the dialogue and put in the other bits afterwards.

♥ Write a consecutive narrative and then insert the dialogue.

♥ Use mind maps. Devised by Tony Buzan (*Use Your Head* and other books), mind maps are a diagrammatical aid to thinking. The writer first writes one key idea or character in the middle of a large sheet of paper and circles it, then branches from that central idea to other circled ideas, writing as quickly and freely as possible. Each separate train of thought is treated as a new branch. Some people use different colours to emphasise different ideas. Many writers find this an extremely useful way of developing character, back story and plot.

Many experienced and multi-published writers always write a complete synopsis or outline for their own use before they begin a book. Others write one when they are stuck and can't figure out where the story is going.

Daphne wrote a chapter outline – one or two sentences per chapter – for her first book so she knew she had enough plot incidents to have something significant happen in each chapter.

When she tried a longer book (a Regency romance) she didn't do that and ended up with a manuscript a little shorter than standard length. This was before word processors, and she confesses to manufacturing an unnecessary plot complication. The first editor astutely recognised this and turned the ms down. A second editor bought it – possibly because she had a slot to fill in a hurry. Don't count on being so lucky, especially in today's tight market.

NB: It is perfectly normal to fall into a hole in the middle of the book, when the story grinds to a halt.

Not knowing this, Robyn wrote half-books for ten years.

Daphne writes through that grinding middle bit, as long-distance runners run through what they call 'the wall'. Robyn found it helps if she writes the last chapter, then fills in the gap. Writing the final scene helps her find out what happened in between.

And no, after being published Robyn didn't finish many of these half-books and sell them. They were works on which she learned her craft – and her limitations. Many were derivative; others had fundamental flaws in technique or plot that made them impossible to sell. And others were simply out of date. Things had changed remarkably in the real world since she'd begun writing; the books that fitted 1965 seemed quaint and old-fashioned in 1975.

Don't let laziness stop you from planning. But if you are a writer who finds a detailed plan, synopsis or chapter outline makes her lose interest in the book because there is nothing left to find out, leave the synopsis until you're finished or nearly so. That synopsis (see p. 85) will be a selling tool, not a writing guide.

Style, voice, tone and mood

Editors may mention these concepts when discussing your manuscript's strengths and flaws.

Voice comes naturally from within the writer. *Style* is a trained voice, honed and refined by technique.

Editors and readers do not want a new Robyn Donald or a new Daphne Clair. They want writers with their own fresh voices. We all learn from other writers, but never smother your own voice by imposing someone else's style on it.

Tone is largely dictated by the story and characters. It can change according to the mood of a specific scene, but each book also has an overall tone. Some are light reading, others darker and more dramatic. In a dark-toned book a deft touch of wry or sophisticated humour can usefully lighten the mood, but a scene of slapstick comedy would probably strike a false note. In a lighter-toned book a scene in which several children die in a road smash would create a dislocation, and the reader may be outraged at this intrusion into the overall tone of the story.

Mood alters according to the emotions expressed in the scene; if the heroine is sad you won't usually describe her feelings in a lighthearted, humorous way. A writer will use different language and a different approach to describing the heroine's first raptures of love from those that show her later disillusion. We do it all the time in speech; you don't describe a funeral in the same way as you describe a party.

We recommend you don't worry about any of these unless an editor comments on them. They are important to the end product, and we do mention them later in the book, but they're not something you should agonise about. Self-consciousness about voice, style and tone can lead to stilted, unnatural, and even pretentious, writing. You can modify or improve these qualities with learned techniques, but it is usually a mistake to make efforts to acquire or transform them.

Other terms common to the trade can be found in general books about writing and publishing. If you plan to make a career in the business, you should read some.

Jargon of the trade

Romantic fiction has its own jargon, and an understanding of this will help you to focus your writing to a particular market – as well as to distinguish the different classifications of romances during your reading:

Genres broad types of popular literature, i.e. romance, mystery, science fiction, fantasy, thriller. Each genre can be subdivided, e.g. a mystery can be a police procedural, an English cosy, a hardboiled private eye, etc. Romances also have subgenres – see further on.

Romances any book in which the progress and eventual resolution of a romance between a man and a woman forms the basic plot. Nowadays, and especially in series romances, the ending is expected to be positive and upbeat, if not comply happy. It would be very hard to sell to an editor a series romance without a positive, upbeat ending where the couple are together for the forseeable future. Many readers would be outraged.

Love stories once synonymous with romance, but increasingly the happy ending is regarded as requisite for 'romance' although a 'love story' may end tragically or ambiguously.

Category romances sometimes referred to as 'series romances'; books aimed at mass market outlets – dairies, supermarkets, etc. – as well as bookshops, and replaced with new stock at usually monthly intervals, much like magazines.

Lines within category, books of similar length, format and cover design (but with individual cover art) printed under an overall 'line name'. Each book within a line is numbered. Several lines may be produced by the same company, varying in length, degree of sensuality, and subject matter (e.g. Mills & Boon Presents, Harlequin Historical, Silhouette Desire). There is often considerable overlap between one line and another.

Usually paperbacks, although some hardcovers may be produced for the library trade.

Library romances usually hardcover, often less tightly focused on romance, more likely to have large parts of the book deal with the heroine's family, job, etc. Not widely sold through bookshops or mass market outlets.

Single title releases novels which are released as individual titles rather than part of a numbered line. More likely to have subplots, extended love scenes, secondary characters. These are usually bigger books – 100,000 words or more. Can be paperback or hardback. Found in airports and mass market outlets as well as in bookstores.

Sensual or sexy romances where the protagonists make love before they are married, and where the love scenes, although not clinically described, are graphic and intense.

Traditional romances (sometimes called 'Sweet') often less than 60,000 words. Protagonists do not usually make love unless they are married, and love scenes are not graphically described. This does not mean the books are insipid, sentimental stories about seventeen-year-old virgins. Traditional romances can deal with controversial subjects and be very intense.

Contemporary set in the present day. Can be short or long, and a single title release or one of a series. High levels of emotional intensity, often sensuous.

Historical series romances with historical settings published as part of a line by specialist publishers or under particular imprints from general publishers.

Historical romances single title releases, often paperback. The protagonists suffer a series of meetings and partings before the happy ending. Tend to be set in 'romantic' periods – mediaeval, Elizabethan, Restoration, Victorian, Edwardian. Subgenres: Viking, American Indian, pirate, Western, American Civil War.

Sagas usually trace the history (romantic, financial and scandalous) of several generations of a family. There may be one or several main protagonists, and one or several love stories involving a central character or a succession of characters.

Regency novels primarily set in the Regency period in England (1812–1820). Comedy of manners harking back to the work of Jane Austen and in the tradition of Georgette Heyer. Some series, some single titles.

Gothics set in any historical period, although the 19th century appears to be the favourite. Woman in danger in large sinister house. Usually she doesn't know which of two men is trying to kill her. Daphne du Maurier's *Rebecca* is a classic of this genre. Considerable crossover with genre below.

Romantic suspense in which suspense plays an important part in the plot and the romance. Series or single title release. If the romance is more important than the suspense, a book will probably be in a category; if the suspense is the main element the book will be a single title.

Futuristic/Fantasy/Paranormal romances in which these elements figure prominently. Angels, vampires, ghosts, fairies, even Death himself have featured. Different lines accept different things. Has much in common with –

Time travel a woman (usually) of the present era is thrown back in time, meets a man with whom she falls in love, and has to decide whether or not to stay in his time. A very popular example is *Cross Stitch* (published as *Outlander* in America) by Diana Gabaldon, the first in a series that has crossed the genre boundaries to become an international mainstream bestseller.

Women's fiction popular novels focused on a central female character or characters. Romantic relationships do not necessarily drive the plot – unlike romances, where it is the particular relationship between one man and one woman that is the heart of the novel.

Glitz longer, single-title releases that concentrate on the lives, loves and spending habits of the very rich and famous and powerful. Focus is usually on a woman, or a small group of women. Hardback and paperback. Also known as 'airport novels'. There may be a strong romance thread but it is not a given and does not drive the story.

Bodice-ripper warning: this term is offensive to writers in every subgenre. Coined to describe 1980s' historical sagas in which the heroine was frequently in danger of rape (true to real life of her times), it is sometimes ignorantly applied to the whole romance genre.

Inspirational romances stories in which one or both protagonists' religious faith (usually Christian) plays an important role in the book.

Young adult romances stories for teenagers; little or no overt sexuality.

Mainstream titles books, often hardback, in which the story is not driven by romance, even if romance is present. There is a blurred division between this and women's fiction (see above).

Breakout book name given to a single title book with which a genre-writer breaks into the mainstream. The term tends to imply that all category writers want to 'break out', but many brilliant writers prefer the challenge of the shorter form.

Lead title the book at the top of the publisher's list. Gets most of the money for publicity, and is expected to sell the most copies. Publishers will try to ensure it does. They have often invested a lot of money in it.

Publisher's list the list of books each publisher produces for the season, or in some cases the month.

2. Characterisation

Characterisation starts with the right name for the character. Names will influence your reader's view of your hero and heroine. (And you probably don't want to call them Slade and Melinda!)

Strong heroes need strong names that define their character. Heroines' names too reflect the kind of person they are. There is a difference between Cecil Wilkinson and Jared Stone, or Kitty Faithfull and Kate Falconer. And between Beth, Lizzie and Elizabeth.

Memorable characters have depth and diversity. They are so vividly portrayed that if your plot forces them to do something against their nature, the reader won't believe it. Plot drives characters – but characters can refuse to obey the dictates of your plot. We find it's best to trust the character and alter the plot rather than force a well-realised character to fit into our pre-conceived plan.

Docile characters who do exactly as you tell them can be dead characters. However, Nabokov, who wrote *Lolita*, said he had no time for characters who 'took over'. His characters did exactly what he told them to do. It may be that he realised his protagonists so vividly that they couldn't do anything out of character.

Building characters

Some writers make a list of things they should know about their characters; it can help to fix them in their minds. They may spend considerable time working up full character sketches before they start writing the book. Other people begin with a plot or an opening situation and think, *What sort of person would behave like that? And why?*

What helps you to see a character? A mind map works well for many writers (see p. 7 for more on mind maps).

You can 'interview' your characters. What is her birthdate or horoscope? His favourite colour? Does she like porridge or muesli? What do they dream about? Their goals in life? And are these really their goals, or do they just think they are?

Some writers use magazine pictures to help them visualise heroes and heroines. You do need to keep details of physical characteristics where you can refer to them, to prevent small slips like having a green-eyed heroine suddenly become brown-eyed in Chapter Nine.

There is no single best way. Many writers need to start writing before they can see their characters clearly, and will discover all they need to know during the writing.

Think about their family backgrounds – what happened to them as children will affect their behaviour in adulthood.

Do they have reason to be confident or suspicious, outgoing or wary of new experiences and new people? If your heroine is a happy, outgoing person and works in public relations, she probably didn't spend her childhood in an isolated, gloomy mansion with a crazed aunt and a sinister, child-hating uncle.

Give the hero and heroine jobs very early, preferably before you start writing. What they do for a living has a direct bearing on their personality, and vice versa. And their personality has a direct bearing on their motivation.

We find that if we know the name, age, any important physical features, the person's job and the setting, we know enough to begin the book. Although we might need to change these first ideas as we write the book.

Defining character for the reader

Character is defined by what they do and say. Does the heroine react to stress by avoidance or by aggression? Does the hero become sarcastic or ominously silent when annoyed? Are they emotionally controlled or volatile? Reserved or bluntly outspoken? Easily provoked or always in control? Placid or quick-tempered?

Don't say the hero is attractive and masterful; show the heroine watching him as he sweeps some lucky woman off her feet while others swoon all around him.

Don't say the heroine is courageous; show her shivering with terror but with her square chin set as she struggles across the ice to protect the baby seal. This also reveals that she's an idealist who is prepared to put up with a considerable amount of discomfort in the furtherance of her ideals.

♥ **Appearance**
   A tall man sees the world differently from a short one, and people will treat him differently. A beautiful woman won't have the same experiences or expectations as a plain one.

♥ **Possessions**
   These also help to illustrate character. Does he live in a mansion or penthouse flat? Drive a Mini or a rakish sports car?

♥ **Clothing**
   Does your heroine wear a skin-tight leather mini and boob-tube, six-inch heels and fishnet stockings? Or a silk blouse, flared skirt and pearls?

♥ **Food**
   Does she drink beer or dry white wine? Does he eat beef curry or rare steak?

All these things help to define your characters as individuals.

Like real people, your characters can display unexpected traits. The woman who goes for power dressing – plain dark suits, sensible heels and disciplined hair – might have a penchant for silk and frills in her underwear. Or the apparently heartless, driving man who has the money to buy all the pedigree dogs he could want, owns a small, timid mutt of doubtful parentage that he rescued from the streets. This tells the reader quite a lot about the hidden parts of a person's character.

The reader may be surprised by what your characters do, but should on reflection be able to see that yes, this man or woman would react that way in those circumstances. If the reader can't believe it, you've lost control of the character.

There is no need to tell the reader everything about your characters in the first chapter; show it in dribs and drabs, using a mixture of dialogue, action and thoughts. Not all of it, just what moves the novel forward, what is vital for the reader to know at this point in this story – which is about falling in love, not about the heroine's career, family or friends. So unless the relationship she had at the age of three with her grandmother is vital for the story, don't bother with it. Everything you write must:

♥ reveal character;

♥ forward the plot; or

♥ depict a mood.

All three if possible. And it quite often is.

Both hero and heroine are strong. They do not just let things happen to them; they are active in their own lives. They don't submit passively to the whims of fate.

Each may be vulnerable, but not weak. A romance is a story of equals, although in high-tension stories it often appears at first that the hero holds all the cards and has the upper hand. A romance is an adventure of the emotions for women, and a powerful adversary makes a much more dramatic situation and ups the stakes on the outcome. It's the David and Goliath story. Would that have been so exciting if David had matched the giant's size and strength?

Like David, many heroines seem to lack the advantages of the hero, but they use their heads (and hearts) and win out in the end.

You must understand your characters well enough to know how they will react to events – certainly by the end of the book, even if you didn't at the beginning. If you are a writer who learns about your characters while you write, you may have to change their earlier reactions once you know them better.

And they must both evolve. A romance novel is really the history of an emotional turning point as your two main characters enter a new life stage, and it is their meeting that triggers it.

They grapple with the problems the writer gives them, growing as they do so.

They discover truths about themselves.

They mature enough to make a commitment to each other, and to a shared future.

Your hero

The hero is for the heroine the embodiment of risk – a crisis point in her life. Even the very quietest, gentlest of heroes must be decisive and effective.

Heroes are invariably considerate to those weaker or less fortunate than themselves. They are never rude to waiters, shop assistants, or anyone who can't answer back. If he's under a misapprehension about her character or actions the hero may treat the heroine with scorn, but even then he behaves with exquisite courtesy. He will open the door for her while hurling dire insults under his breath. He will not embarrass her in public. Even if he grew up on the wrong side of the tracks he has learned his manners somewhere along the way. (And later in the book, after discovering how wrong he is about her, he will recant, retract, and *grovel* very nicely.)

If he's inclined to be masterful he must have cause and he should not be petty with it. Show his strength of character in action scenes, don't just talk about it. He is capable, a leader, but not perfect. He may have a fiery temper, or suffer from jealousy or distrust, but if he is bitter and angry there must be a valid reason – preferably other than some woman done him wrong!

Robyn creates tough, hard, dominant (*not* domineering) heroes who often fall apart emotionally the first time they see the heroine (but never let her know it!) and who eventually realise that this is the only woman they'll ever love.

Heroes these days do not assume they have a right to punish the heroine for leading a man (himself or another) on. They do not ask the heroine to give up her career for marriage. They never rape or explicitly threaten to do so. And they never hit or physically hurt her.

Some of the male attitudes common in an earlier generation which were depicted or somewhat exaggerated in romances of their time aren't acceptable now. A hero can be rugged, harsh, fierce, obdurate and ruthless, but he is capable of softer emotions. Even the harshest heroes are redeemable.

The hero is a threat to the heroine's peace of mind, to her way of life, as often she is to his. Robyn likes a hero to be strong yet vulnerable – and to be ready to die rather than let anyone, especially the heroine, see how vulnerable he is.

You might like gentle, kind heroes, and that's fine. But readers don't want heroes who are wimps. You need to be very careful with your characterisation and motivations. If he's too nice and sympathetic your readers are going to say, 'This heroine is a fruitcake. Any woman with half an ounce of grey matter would snatch up this wonderful man and rush him post-haste to the nearest marriage celebrant.'

Even a good-humoured hero subtly threatens to disrupt the heroine's carefully ordered life. Gentle heroes are usually large and protective, and sometimes have an endearing bumbling quality. Part of their appeal is that their obvious physical strength is at the service of the heroine, not turned against her. At the same time they are successful in their own field, whatever it may be. They are competent human beings and worth-

19

while members of society. Some writers even have their hero make foolish mistakes and look stupid on occasion, but it is only temporary. Basically they handle themselves well.

The hero is not necessarily more sexually experienced than the heroine, although that is still acceptable. Rakes, however, are no longer hero material in this age of AIDS.

Heroes are secure in their sexuality and are often frank about their sexual feelings for the heroine. Above all else, their honest desire to please the heroine makes them excellent lovers.

The hero is sexy, at least to the heroine, though not always immediately or obviously. There have been heroes who can't see without their glasses, heroes who are not handsome or charismatic, who do not have glamorous jobs or lots of money. Some are blind or lame, scarred or confined to a wheelchair.

Each hero has his own strengths and weaknesses. A gentle knight has to convince his lady that she can have all she wants out of life, and him too; convince her that he is the only man for her – something he knows instinctively – even though he may at times have self-doubts. An overprotective hero must be prepared to allow the heroine her independence.

Your heroine should sense that she is the only person who has such a powerful effect on him, just as he is the only man who can make her reassess the foundations on which she has built her life until the moment they met. She is able to read (because you have written them) the small signs that tell her (and the reader) that he is trustworthy even though he may be pretending to be an enemy agent; or that the toughness and antagonism which so repel her at first are only the outward indications of a man afraid to make himself vulnerable by falling in love.

A hero tries to behave honourably. His allegiance to another person or his country may lead to less than perfect behaviour, but it always bothers him. And where he is driven to act badly by his overwhelming feelings for the heroine he's appalled.

He treats the heroine with consideration, even when he is angry with her. If she looks tired he sends her home in a taxi.

If she turns pale he finds a chair. He notices her; he is, after all, falling in love – or already in love – with her.

The heroine knows at some instinctive level that she can trust him, because the writer has given him at least one scene in which he is revealed as trustworthy and honourable. Robyn's heroes are often men who admit to being difficult to live with, who demand extremely high standards in every aspects of their lives. They are take-charge men with family responsibilities, men whose faults are likely to be manifestations of strength and power.

Many of Daphne's heroes are loners hiding wounds to their souls, wearing a mask of control because they don't trust themselves to be good husbands and fathers.

Your hero will be different from ours, just as our particular kinds of heroes probably wouldn't have much in common if they met.

A hero is a success on his own terms, which may not fit those of society. He will be well on the way to achieving his goals in both life and career. Often authoritative, he's not perfect, but a true hero has a sense of compassion and the capacity to love.

Your heroine

The heroine often has to overcome obstacles and dangers, fight the dragon (i.e. overcome the male hero's sometimes angry resistance and/or conquer her own fears) to gain what she wants – equality in a loving male-female relationship.

She may have emotional problems which lead her to distrust the hero or men in general. However, she will overcome these as she learns to trust the hero.

While she should be sensible and not silly, she can make mistakes, be vulnerable, have moments when she snarls at the cat. Like the hero, she should be a competent person, not forever needing to be rescued.

There must be an inner logic to her thoughts and behaviour, a logic based on her character and background. You don't want your reader to say, 'Nobody in their right mind would behave like that!'

The heroine, certainly by the end of the book, will stand on her own feet, be able to face down the hero (or anyone else) and be a true partner in their relationship. The hero may not at first recognise her inner strength, but it is there.

Your heroine may have a high-powered job, be rich in her own right and be a success in her own career, and she does not these days sacrifice everything for the hero. She may feel that her career or her self-respect or her independence are not worth giving up for a man. But although she can live without him, she goes through agony when they're apart. In the end she freely chooses to share her life with the hero; she is not forced to do so by society or other outside pressures, and certainly not by him.

It may be that she feels her career or her life plans are endangered by her love for him, or she has been so deeply hurt in the past she's vowed never to be vulnerable to any man again. She may acknowledge her love quite frankly, but feel that loyalty to someone else – a family member, boss, bene-factor – has priority over her own and the hero's happiness. Her job or other loyalties may force her to withhold her trust because so far it's only based on emotion, not verifiable facts. Or she may be convinced that she is bad news for the hero; or conversely, she may ardently pursue a committed relationship with an emotionally scarred hero who believes she will be hurt by loving him.

She doesn't need to have a blinding flash of revelation on page 185 that what she thought was hate was really love mas-querading under another guise.

Heroines sometimes find it necessary to assert their inde-pendence. They may argue, fight and stand up for their rights and the rights of others, but if they are always thinking the worst of a well-meaning man – forever jumping on him for no good reason, throwing tantrums when the poor guy is obvi-ously doing his best in the circumstances – they come across as immature, bad-tempered shrews. Readers will not like them.

A heroine listens to reason rather than going off half-cocked every time the hero opens his mouth. If she misunderstands his motives or actions she has a logical reason.

Beware of plots that rely solely on misperceptions; the reader will lose patience with this idiot woman and apparently masochistic man. Any man who continues to court a woman who has spurned him every time he approaches her runs the risk of looking like either a doormat or a sexual harasser.

Although a heroine may behave badly on occasion or hide her inner scars from the world and from the hero under an icy or angry façade, the reader must sense that underneath this distant or antagonistic mask is a damaged creature who has a believable motivation for resisting her attraction to a wonderful man who is obviously made for her.

The heroine should always observe the normal courtesies of life; you don't want your readers muttering that her parents should have taught her better manners.

Your heroine knows that her powerful initial attraction to the hero is almost entirely sexual. She understands that there is much more to love than this, and she is not going to bestow herself and her future on the hero until she is sure there is more to their relationship than sex, and that he too realises it.

Choose scenes and events to provide your hero and heroine with opportunities to overcome the obstacles you have put in their path and deepen their love and trust in ways consistent with their characters.

At the end of the book make it clear that the heroine – and the reader – can trust this man with her life, her wellbeing, and eventually her children. The real threat, which she has finally come to see is no threat, is in her own emotional vulnerability to the appeal of the hero.

Secondary characters

Secondary characters can be sketched in with a telling but brief phrase or sentence.

They are in your book for a reason, but the reader shouldn't get too emotionally involved with them. They need not be as deeply understood, or as well rounded as the main characters. Let them do their bit to help the story along, then send them off to the wings to wait for their next cue.

Because minor characters may be off the page for some time, a particular character tag will help the reader identify them when they turn up again:

> Owen Armstrong leaned against the window... His tall, thin frame was loosely encased in a brown suit with a blue shirt, and his tie as usual was both unsuitable and askew.
>
> Stella blinked at the green-on-yellow pattern of what appeared to be a species of slightly deformed pine tree, and hastily averted her eyes to the Company Secretary's long, intelligent face. (p.6, *Take Hold of Tomorrow*, Daphne Clair)
>
> Later in the day Owen wandered into her office and sat fingering his tie, a wide one today with a violet sunburst design superimposed on silver and blue stripes, that clashed wonderfully with his mustard-coloured shirt and green tweed jacket. (p.95, *Take Hold of Tomorrow*)

Walk-on characters don't need to be named or drawn at all – the waiter who serves dinner is merely a bit player. However, if he has any other part in the story he should have some sort of personality, and if he's going to appear again he definitely needs to be characterised with a pithy, memorable phrase, so your reader doesn't say, 'Hang on, who's this person? Oh, the waiter from Chapter Two? I didn't know he was going to turn up again.'

If a new character pops up every second page or so, with a new name to be thought out, a new characteristic, see if you can't combine several of them into one person. Especially in a short category romance, you simply don't have enough space for more than a few minor characters – probably about six at the most.

Even in a saga or a big historical too many characters confuse the reader, more so if too many of them are on the page at once. Don't overload your story with a cast of thousands.

Minor characters shouldn't run away with the story. Sometimes the heroine's best friend turns out to be funnier/smarter/more interesting than the heroine. Remove her forthwith.

If she's so darned fascinating give her her own romance – when you've finished with this one. The amusingly eccentric aunt, too, or the sweet little four-year-old, can have the most encroaching ways. Before you know where you are you've written a chapter where neither the hero nor the heroine show up. Be ruthless with secondary characters.

It sounds rather obvious, but if they're not promoting the plot, what on earth are they doing cluttering up your pages?

3. Motivation and Source of Tension

Why is the heroine wandering through a graveyard at midnight in her nightgown when she knows there's a vampire on the loose?

If it's necessary for the plot, if she has to be there, then you had better give her an excellent, totally watertight reason. That she felt the need for a breath of fresh air is not enough.

If you can't come up with that reason, then no matter how wonderfully you've written the scene, no matter how necessary it is to your plot, no matter how deliciously your reader's blood is going to curdle, you'll have to think again.

In a novel people must behave in a way that's consistent with their characters. No sensible heroine would risk her life in a vampire-infested cemetery, unless her children were in mortal danger *and* she was festooned with small crosses and garlic cloves and armed with a rifle and 100 assorted silver bullets, the graveyard was at the crossroads, and she had laid in a supply of stakes.

Give the heroine a good, logical, emotionally satisfying motivation for everything she does and everything she says – a reason that seems inevitable, not contrived or false.

Even if your heroine doesn't always understand the hero's motivation you, the writer, must. And the reader should know or at least guess that he has a credible motivation for everything he does and says.

It's perilously easy to further your plot by writing a scene in which the hero is rude to the heroine. Unfortunately, in the next scene he must nudge the plot onward again by kissing her. Thus is born the famous weathervane hero; without motivation for his actions, he simply swings in the wind, waiting vacantly for another plot twist to give him a shove in the right direction.

Behaviour stems from character and circumstances.

Know what the characters are thinking and feeling – and why – and their behaviour will ring true.

If the hero is being insulting and rude to a perfectly normal, sane, attractive young woman who has never done him any harm, or if a supposedly intelligent heroine freezes off a strong, intelligent, good-looking, successful, right-minded and basically kind-hearted hero, what on earth is the matter with them? Are they crazy?

A passerby's polite offer to help a fellow motorist in trouble does not warrant the heroine snapping, 'Back off, you arrogant, overbearing male chauvinist.'

Seeing a woman talking to someone of racy reputation will not logically lead a man to believe she is a slut, and even less does it entitle him to treat her as something he would like to wipe from his shoes. This kind of thing stems from a writer's attempt to fabricate conflict instead of setting up a situation and delineating characters from which romantic tension will naturally arise.

Don't have Slade and Melinda react in extreme ways to trivial circumstances, or swing wildly between black moods and happy ones, between gentle and aggressive behaviour, unless you can convey to the reader what has caused the sudden change and make it seem perfectly understandable.

Minor conflicts have their roots in some major internal tension in the character which the reader will identify with. Manufacturing tension or conflict out of nothing indicates a desperate writer forcing her characters into implausible behaviour.

You are not writing about manic-depressives. These are normal, mature people (even if young in years), who are caught up in something that they may not have experienced before and that is about to alter their entire lives.

So how will they react to this sudden kick of fate? What kinds of people are they? What influences formed their

27

personalities? Feed in small bits of background so the reader understands why they are reacting this way.

The more thoroughly you know your characters, the more rounded and believable they will be, and the more credible your plot twists become (see Characterisation, p.14).

Characters do not act and react in a vacuum on some arbitrary whim of the author, or because 'romantic heroes/heroines act this way'. There must be some underlying reason, some character logic.

A clearly formulated source of tension will help you create characters who are consistent and believable.

The opening situation

Opening situations should not be confused with the source of tension. The hero mistaking the heroine for a prostitute, the heroine expecting a female housekeeper and getting a male one, the hero being convinced the heroine is a conniving bitch who done his brother or himself wrong, are *opening situations*.

An opening situation gets the couple together.

Sometimes this is all you have when you start a book, but an opening situation does not make a story. A misunderstanding can seldom sustain an entire book. What is the hero's attitude to prostitutes, and why? Why is the heroine so against the idea of a male housekeeper? How come the hero is so suspicious of women? Answer these questions and you may have a source of tension.

Source of tension

The source of tension is the core of your story. It stops a book from being a collection of scenes and turns it into a novel.

Tension keeps the reader in a state of suspense, even though she knows the guy in the white hat will win the gunfight, the murderer will be found, the lovers will live happily ever after.

Tension or conflict drives the story and motivates the characters – the irresistible force meeting the immovable object. In romantic fiction the primary tension is essentially an emotional one, with a covert or overt edge of sexual awareness between the couple. External tensions may be present, but these are not the main plot, although they can play a part as plot twists or subplots to further the story.

A love story is basically a story about feelings, and the action is generated by the emotions experienced by the characters. This is in direct contrast to most male romance (genre fiction such as westerns, thrillers, etc.), which relies heavily on action, and where emotions are largely a reaction to external forces.

In women's romances tension arises from the attraction/resistance dynamics between the hero and heroine.

Some stories are about people who fall in love gently and without fireworks, but who may distrust their own ability to make the other person happy because of their previous experience or because of social pressures. And gifted writers have generated tension from the normal uncertainties of falling in love and getting to know each other more deeply. Committing one's life, happiness and future children to the keeping of another person is to gamble one's entire future, after all!

But if a couple meet, fall in love on page one and get married at the end of Chapter One, while it may be nice it is not a story. Stories are built on tension.

Remember, tension arises from character and situation.

The writer must let the reader know why Melinda and Slade can't just fall in love and live happily ever. If it would spoil your story to spell out the reasons in the first chapter, you must still lay the trail with hints early in the book, letting the reader know that Hey, something interesting is going on here, and it's worthwhile reading on to find out what it is.

The stronger the *source* of the tension, the more potential for emotional intensity there is.

Melinda and Slade may have had an explosive previous relationship that remains unresolved so they are afraid of further pain. One may think that the other has done something nasty to someone they are fond of, or feels that the other has betrayed them in the past.

Give them something that can't be resolved by any sensible person in five minutes. The best sources of tension appear at first to be absolutely unresolvable.

Don't exasperate the reader by making a big thing out of some small incident. If one character asking a simple, direct question would fix all their problems the plot is based on a very flimsy premise, and readers will know it.

Make sure your characters are not being totally unreasonable and unfair, and not acting stupidly – seeing insults where none exist, or never giving the other party a reasonable chance to explain.

Tension is not bickering. A series of squabbles does not make a story. Neither does a series of love scenes. And alternating them doesn't do it either.

The main obstacle has to be serious enough to keep sensible people apart – that the hero doesn't like red hair is not enough, unless perhaps his mother had long red hair and tried to strangle him with it when he was six. And it must be important enough to sustain the tension for at least 50,000 and maybe up to 100,000 words.

A heroine continually wondering, 'Does he really love me?' is not going to produce a lot of intensity, and the reader is likely to become irritated with the thinness of the story. But if Melinda has to ask herself, 'Is this man capable of really loving *anyone*?' you are getting at the source of the tension. The reader will wonder *why* Slade seems incapable of this basic human emotion. And it's the writer's job to provide the answer in a way that the reader will accept and understand.

The longer you can keep Melinda and Slade from solving their problems – and the reader on tenterhooks – the better.

Don't bend, twist or maim your characters so that they will fit your plot. A source of tension which is forced on unlikely

30

characters or suddenly revealed without any warning and without clues being laid beforehand is a form of manipulation, one the reader sees through and resents.

The more clearly you understand the source of tension the more likely it is that the story will flow in a logical progression from start to finish without major rewriting. That said, there are times when the source of tension is difficult to identify, and both of us have occasionally not recognised it until we were well into writing the book.

Tension arises within or between *people* – a woman who was a rape victim and the man who marries her; a woman who falls in love with the man who killed her father; a man who is afraid to love and the woman who loves him; a woman who is strong and independent and a man who is strong and protective.

The heroine's suspicion that the hero murdered his first wife is a strong source of tension. Asking him if he did so will not resolve the tension, since a murderer is presumed capable of lesser sins like lying.

Finding the hero in another woman's arms is not a strong source of tension unless the author comes up with a cast-iron, believable reason why the heroine can't just ask him what he was doing there. It may be a minor plot point but it will not carry a novel.

Disagreements may flare up over small things, but it must be clear that these differences are only a symptom of the real issue between the main characters because the more impossible it gets for them to commit to each other, the more tense they are.

Each scene has to build the tension or lay the groundwork for the next buildup of tension, using both character development and action.

The source of tension is the engine of your novel – it drives the plot, and is the basis of the excitement, the sexual tension and the romance.

If the engine dies – if the source of tension is resolved before the final chapter – you will then have to introduce another. There will be a limp patch and the reader will suspect that you ran out of ideas before you ran out of pages, and you lose their willing suspension of disbelief.

The resolution

The primary tension of all love stories is the emotional threat or danger perceived by the characters. This must be faced and overcome.

Resolution of the tension is not achieved by some outside force or sudden enlightenment, although these may be factors allowing Slade and Melinda to achieve greater self-knowledge and understanding of their relationship. Ideally it is brought about by their personal growth which allows them to understand and accept themselves and each other.

You have laid the groundwork for the resolution throughout, so that like every other plot twist it seems logical and even inevitable – but not until the moment of revelation. The conclusion must satisfy the reader, not have her thinking, 'But wait a minute – didn't he... and wasn't she...? No, I don't believe it!'

The resolution should imply that the two protagonists have a future together and that they are committed to a relationship. It does not have to promise wedding bells, unmitigated bliss and happy-ever-after.

It can hint at major problems still ahead, but should leave the reader feeling that these two people have already overcome seemingly insurmountable obstacles and that they have everything going for them now. They will win through because they are both strong, sensible, capable and mature people – equals who care passionately for each other and will support each other to the hilt.

4. Structure, Plots and subplots

Structure

The classic structure is:

♥ 1: establish the status quo and introduce conflict (which we prefer to call tension);

♥ 2: show the effects of the tension; and

♥ 3: resolve the tension and show how it has changed the status quo.

Start your story when *things are about to change.*

The agent of change that will trigger the source of tension into action should be introduced as soon as possible. Often this is the hero, striding in to disrupt the heroine's nicely predictable life.

You can sketch in the status quo quite quickly, leaving details to be filled in later.

If the heroine owns a business you don't have to tell the reader on page one – or even in Chapter One – that she inherited it from her father, that he really wanted a son, that she spent her childhood trying to live up to his expectations, that he was a hard man who treated her mother badly, that she has vowed never to marry because she doesn't want to be a slave and a drudge to any man...

In a short romance it is almost essential, and in a longer one nearly always best, to introduce the hero or heroine on the first page, and if possible both. And do it without slowing the pace (see p. 46).

Here you need only one or two physical characteristics, a

general idea of mood and character, and enough of the setting to tell us where the scene takes place.

Don't bog the reader down with details. The colour of the kitchen walls, the hum of the computers on half a dozen desks, the hiss of tyres on the wet road may be all you need to set the scene. If the setting is extremely important you can include other information later. If not, we all know roughly what a kitchen, a business office or a city street looks like.

Treat everything on a need-to-know basis. Readers trust you to give them necessary information at the appropriate time, and the way to keep them interested is to involve them in the characters' emotions *as things happen.*

Emotion without action soon becomes boring, and so does action without emotion. And setting without either is the fastest way to a cure for insomnia.

Narrative

Narrative (the simplest story form) is 'and then and then...' or, 'This happened and then that happened and then...' This may be a series of random events, told chronologically.

Plot

Plot is And then, *but* then, *so* then: 'This happened and then because this happened, that happened...' It is action and reaction, a logical chain of events, twisting in unexpected ways but moving towards the satisfying conclusion.

Your plot will create an obstacle course for the characters. They have a goal (lasting happiness together) which is frustrated by a formidable source of tension and other smaller, related difficulties. A good plot furnishes an insurmountable problem, and then solves it in a satisfying manner.

Plot is not always revealed chronologically. Writers use techniques such as flashbacks, changing points-of-view and dialogue rather than straight narration, to further or complicate the unravelling of the plot.

Subplots

Subplots grow out of character and the main plot, and may involve minor characters. Watch for potential subplots which will interconnect with the main plot and affect the lives of the main characters. Subplots add richness and texture. But if they don't affect the main plot or if they take over the book they are not doing their job properly.

The subplot may be someone else's love story (the other woman, the heroine's friend, the other man, or the heroine's mother etc.) It may be a family mystery or a career glitch. Whatever it is, the subplot grows out of the circumstances the protagonists find themselves in.

A subplot in a romance novel must not be allowed to take the tension from the main story, but should in some way add to it. Short category romances have little room for fully developed subplots. Longer books can carry them and may indeed need a subplot or subplots to maintain tension and depth.

Remember 'And... but... so.'

A man and woman meet, *and* are attracted, *but* something stops them getting together, *so*...

The pattern is repeated in different scenes throughout the story, not as isolated incidents or misunderstandings, but as a cumulative series of events based on a strong source of tension and building to a climax and eventual resolution.

Plot devices

A warning – writers sometimes write their plots into a corner, where there is no way out for the characters except for some-one – e.g. an inconvenient wife or husband – to fortuitously die, or some outsider to the central plot to arrive and fix things, like a fairy godmother. Be wary of either of these devices, as they are regarded by many readers as 'cheating', and such an ending may leave them dissatisfied.

If you must use something like this, make sure the fairy godmother already has a part in the story and a penchant for interfering, that the inconvenient wife has a dicky heart, or the husband is habitually a drunk driver.

In other words, set it up beforehand. Instead of a glaring plot device, the timely intervention or demise then becomes a logical outcome. However, a fairy godmother should only provide the impetus for the two characters to resolve their problem themselves. Next time she may not be around.

Theme

For some people the concept of a central theme is useful to hold the plot together. 'Theme' is generally expressed as a central idea that may be stated in one word or a short phrase – the theme of Othello is jealousy. Crime Doesn't Pay is a theme.

Every romance is about two people learning to love and trust each other, so the overall theme of any romance is Love Conquers All. However, each individual story has a specific theme – perhaps jealousy, pride, divided loyalty – that grows out of the characters.

Although some writers won't start a book until they identify its theme, and books have been begun with nothing more than a strong theme in the writer's mind, for neither of us is it necessary. We feel that concentrating on a specific source of tension is more helpful.

Like all writing techniques, theme is a tool. Use it if it works for you.

Building blocks

Scenes

A scene shows one or more events occurring in a continuous time-frame. Scenes are the building blocks of novels. They dramatise the answer to the reader's all-consuming question, 'What happened next?'

In each scene something must happen, must change, however subtly. Characters move from indifference to interest, from happiness to despair, from ignorance to knowledge, or at the very least the reader gains a new insight into one or both main characters.

Every important story event needs a scene, which may be as short as a paragraph or as long as a chapter – or even several chapters. Events that took place before the story began may need a scene too. This is the reason for flashbacks.

Intensely emotional passages – the ones that lead to a change in attitude – are usually described fully.

The more momentous the scene, the more detail you use – and the more carefully you have to choose those details – because this is one of the things that indicates heightened awareness. The reader subconsciously picks up that something vital is going on. By detail we mean what your viewpoint character (the character on whose shoulder you are sitting – see p. 51) can see, hear, smell, feel and taste – the clues that reveal what each character is really thinking as opposed to what they are saying, that reveal the emotions they are trying to hide.

Be sure that every scene introduces some new element – something that the *reader* and perhaps the *characters* didn't know before.

Between scenes give necessary information as succinctly as possible using:

Narrative
Relating minor story events that the reader needs to know, such as how a person got from A to B, or what made her late for her crucial appointment, or how much time elapsed between her first meeting with the hero and her second.

Exposition
Explaining what sort of person a character is, how he/she feels, or how something works. Note that passages detailing the heroine's sexual feelings toward the hero and vice versa are exposition and should be used sparingly when nothing is actually happening.

Description
Telling the reader what a person looks like or describing the setting in which the action takes place. Use in small doses, not large chunks.

Give scenes more weight – and much, much more page space – than any of the above.

If you have more than ten lines of narrative ask yourself if this is important enough to show the reader in a scene. Or should it be told through dialogue between the characters? (But don't use dialogue to give static information that both characters already know, or that isn't important to them.)

You do not need a scene to describe how someone got from the house to the bus stop, or even from Turkestan to the Antarctic. That can be done in a sentence or two:

> She was glad to get on the plane and away from the dust and heat of the tropics, but three days later she wished she could have transported some of that heat to the South Pole.

On every page aim for more action and dialogue than narrative, and in every chapter make sure the proportion of dialogue and action (scenes) is vastly higher than the narrative and exposition sequences.

'Actions' need not be large and obvious. A kiss on the cheek or a deliberate turning away from someone is an action. Every action of your characters must tell the reader something about their emotions at the time, and even very small actions can give a lot of information and be a dramatic turning point.

In the old Garbo film *Camille* one of the most intense moments is when Camille drops her fan. The villain tells her she has dropped it and waits for her to pick it up. The hero picks it up and hands it to her. The villain's contempt, the heroine's humiliation and heartbreak, the hero's hurt, anger, love and fundamental decency are all revealed in those few moments. And most importantly, the central relationship subtly shifts to another plane.

A great scene about a car crash where the heroine saves a dozen people may be wonderfully done, but if it doesn't advance the story it doesn't belong in the book.

If the hero is a racing driver and she sees what a crash might do to him and decides that she can't face it, leading her to break off the relationship, then it belongs. If he's a trauma-team doctor or a paramedic and she begins to understand why he got furious with her when she drove too fast just for fun, then it belongs.

If the hero thought she was a brainless blonde incapable of doing anything useful, and he realises how badly he under-estimated her, then it belongs.

The climax

Build gradually to a climax.

The climax is a necessary, dramatic, intense scene which cannot be avoided. In some books you may need to keep a vital piece of information for this important scene. If you fill the reader in too far beforehand – especially on something the hero or heroine doesn't know – your climactic scene can fall very flat. So do give clues and hints if there is to be some big revelation, but try to keep something back.

The climax may lead straight to the resolution – also an obligatory and intensely dramatic scene which the reader sub-consciously expects and must not be cheated of. Or it can be separated from the resolution by the Dark Night of the Soul.

The Dark Night

Also known as the Black Moment, this is the period between the climactic scene when all seems doomed – when Melinda and Slade realise there is no chance of a happy ending for them – and the moment one or both of them takes the first hesitant step towards a resolution of their problems.

In earlier romances the Dark Night sometimes took up a whole chapter but even if it lasts a year in real time, a page is often enough to cover this period in a short book. It is a time of great pain for the protagonists but also a time of growth and revelation. During the dark night of the soul both discover that although pride or circumstances make their happiness seem out of reach, they are strong enough to overcome that pride, to fight and face the consequences of the circumstances that forced them apart.

Melinda and Slade's recognition that they can resolve their source of tension comes from within, and the writer should make sure that it is credible for these characters; it should not be imposed from outside 'because the ending has to be happy in a romance'.

Think about your characters very carefully, and choose incidents – or trains of thought – that fit them.

When they have had their epiphany, their flash of insight, of understanding, then set them back on the path towards the final resolution and that positive, upbeat ending they now deserve, because they have grown and matured enough to make the compromises that will lead to happiness.

Resolution

Try to tie up minor loose ends before the last chapter, unless resolving the major tension will automatically resolve the minor ones.

The resolution is the last big scene, when everything is resolved and Slade and Melinda are able to look forward to a life together. It must involve *both protagonists*, just as the final battle in an action movie has to pit the hero against the villain. You have set up an expectation and must not disappoint your reader.

It is a writing class dictum that the resolution should be got over with as quickly as possible after the climax. Daphne once startled an audience of English teachers by pointing out that this is a very masculine doctrine. 'You can see where that came from!' she told them, drawing in the air the steep rise and fall pattern of a 'male climax', and causing a stunned silence followed by roars of laughter as she illustrated the 'typical' female climax in similar fashion.

Women's climaxes tend to be less precipitous. In women's books the resolving of the emotional issues triggered at the climax can take some time. Sometimes (though not always) the climax of a romantic novel occurs not long after halfway, and working towards the final resolution may take several chapters. But there will be another big scene close to the end to bring about the resolution.

This scene can't be just another misunderstanding cleared up. One or both of the lovers must have experienced some revelation, an epiphany of understanding of either themselves or the other protagonist. This may be triggered by outside forces – near-fatal accidents used to be popular – but the revelation or understanding is an interior thing, a fundamental change in the person.

The book should end when the tension is resolved, when the lovers can make a commitment to a shared future. Here you must be careful neither to finish too abruptly nor limply trail off. Work to make your ending as strong and satisfying as the rest of the book.

Chapters

Chapters can be as long or short as you need, but it helps to aim at 15-, 20- or 30-page chapters in your first draft so you have some idea how you are progressing.

Dramatic events or developments make good chapter ends, but manufactured cliff-hangers can jar. Although your chapter endings should be strong or satisfying, not a lame hanging thread, you're not writing a thriller. You can end a chapter in the middle of a scene or dialogue passage to emphasise an important turning point or to give what could seem a throw-away line a greater significance.

First and last chapters are sometimes markedly shorter than others. The first chapter may be little more than a hook (see pp. 111–112), and sometimes a short last chapter is needed to tie up loose ends or reassure the reader that the hero and heroine are indeed happy and fulfilled. If the heroine is pregnant at the end of the book, it is almost obligatory to tell the reader in a short final scene about the safe arrival of the baby, its sex and its name.

Prologues and epilogues

A prologue (at the beginning) or epilogue (at the end) is actually a short chapter describing an event or events separated in time from the main time span of the book.

A prologue gives necessary information on what happened before the story opens. It may be useful in a 'five years after' book. It may be told from a different point of view than the rest of the book.

An epilogue is a reassurance for the reader that some secondary problem or subsequent important event that the book cannot encompass is ultimately resolved satisfactorily – for example stepchildren, unwelcoming in-laws, competing careers.

Occasionally an epilogue is used to tease the reader into reading a sequel or following book in a series by setting up a bridging scene between the two stories, involving characters from both.

Once upon a time...
Classic romance plot situations

Cinderella • working woman meets millionaire; or its variation, the secretary-boss situation – now sometimes with the sexes reversed.

The woman with everything • she has her career, friends, money of her own, but he can give her the one thing missing, the Love of a Good Man. He must show her that he can emotionally enhance her life.

Amnesia • heroine has lost her memory (or sometimes it's the hero). A chance to start life anew. Perhaps related to –

The Sleeping Beauty • she is unawakened or has withdrawn after being emotionally injured, and only he can awaken or heal her.

Man alone • similar to above. He has retired from society, vowing never to love again. Writer must provide strong motivation for this.

The teacher/mentor • hero helps the heroine become educated, confident and sophisticated. Or mentors a talented woman to fulfil her potential. Not very common now. Women make it on their own. It has been used in reverse in modern romances, with the woman as mentor or teacher.

The virgin and the rake • AIDS put paid to this one, except in a very muted form.

Marriage of convenience • making a relationship work from an unpromising beginning. Strangers marrying.

Forced marriage • hero coerces the heroine into marriage, but then repents and must woo her. Hard to do in modern times, but a challenge! (see variations below)

Pluto and Persephone • kidnapped, downed in the jungle, caught in no-man's-land with a dangerous male. Subgenres include American Indian romances and pirate romances. Closely related to –

Revenge • the heroine wants the hero to fall in love with her in order to avenge a sister/friend/herself, and gets hoist with her own petard; can be reversed, with the hero bent on revenge, but difficult to make him a sympathetic protagonist.

The governess/nanny • healing a dysfunctional family. Gentle newcomer brings happiness to an unhappy household. Often combined with –

Leaving home • young woman finds herself, and in doing so finds love.

Five years after • often combined with hidden child plot. Love affair/marriage went wrong, couple gets a second chance.

False incest • one of the couple (not usually both) believes or suspects they are nearly related.

He only wants my body • or thinks he does! Very classic but a bit thin on its own.

The healing heroine • heroine emotionally heals the physically or mentally scarred hero. Damaged, bitter heroes used to be quite popular. Sometimes reversed.

Dual career • hero and heroine's career paths seem incompatible. Who is going to compromise?

Hidden child • past love affair resulting in a child which the father wasn't told about. The father turns up and upsets the heroine's carefully organised life.

Surrogate mother • hero wants a child but not a wife, and heroine is the surrogate mother chosen. Or the surrogate regrets giving up the child and goes looking for contact. Several variations on the theme.

The mistress • the heroine is the successful hero's traditional-type mistress who succeeds in becoming his wife.

5. Pace and Focus

Pace

Pace is the speed at which story events happen, the combination of action and plot that keeps the reader turning the pages.

In a romance, action is not necessarily a man being chased by a woman in black leather along a steel girder forty feet above the ground. It may be a man meeting a woman in a shop. Or a woman looking at a man. Much of the action involves the subtle growth of relationships.

Romances are about people in a state of heightened awareness; small details and incidents are important and significant, the action and emotion inextricably intertwined. In fact, action could be said to be dramatised emotion.

One of the things that stops people reading is pages and pages when nothing seems to happen – long passages of description or introspection, or scenes where the characters rush around doing things but their relationship doesn't progress.

At the beginning of *The Colour of Midnight* Robyn wrote a great mood piece – atmospheric, dripping with resonance, entirely suited to the plot, and with quite a lot of back story tucked into it. Six pages.

Her editor said, 'Six pages with no dialogue is too long.'

'It's good,' Robyn protested.

'It reads well,' her editor answered cautiously. 'However, it holds up the pace.'

So Robyn cut it to two pages. And held her breath until the

editor said, 'Well, all right, although two pages without dialogue is one too many.'

The editor, of course, was quite right. A slow lead-in bores readers. '*Get on with it*', they mutter, flicking through the pages to see where the book really starts.

Those first few pages draw the reader into your book. Begin as close to the moment of impact – of meeting – as you can.

Once you begin, keep the story moving. In every scene introduce some new element, something that the characters or the reader didn't know before.

Use lots of dialogue (see pp. 64–70), and make sure it pushes the story forward. Dialogue speeds the pace when the reader is learning new things from it.

The way you handle dialogue can speed up or slow down the pace of a scene. Long speeches slow the pace. They should only be used in highly emotional passages, if at all.

Time

The action in a short category romance usually takes place over a matter of weeks or months, although the back-story may be set five or ten years ago, which is when you use flashbacks. Flashbacks too early in the book can slow the pace. Use them only when the reader has enough information to make her anxious to discover what events of months or years ago are affecting the characters now.

In a short novel that drags on over a long period the story may become bogged down. A longer book can take a longer time span but it still needs to move. Very big books are often divided into segments, sometimes with years between them which are skipped over.

If you race through the novel without stopping for breath the reader will feel like a disappointed tourist driven non-stop and far too quickly through a glorious landscape. Conversely, if nothing changes your tourist will feel as though she's been staring out of the windscreen at the same airport carpark for ever.

Pacing your scenes

When you've finished the first draft of your novel check out your important turning points when things change dramatically. Make sure you've given these scenes their due weight, their colour and their power.

Every scene has its individual pace. In crucial scenes skilfully chosen details will slow the pace but increase the tension, indicating to the reader that something momentous is about to happen.

If you whisk your reader through a vital scene without giving her time to absorb its significance she may think, 'Hey, wait a minute. How did Melinda say that? Why is she so alarmed? Just what sort of look did Slade give her when she snapped at him?'

No novel should be all white water, or all calm sunlit reaches. Check that your big scenes aren't clumped together; a ferocious argument might need to be followed by reverie. However, interior monologue notoriously slows pace. While your heroine is mourning the fact that she is wildly in love with the hero although he's still calling her Miss Um-Aah, the action stops. So give her something to do while she's thinking. Her actions can echo her thoughts:

> How could he have flirted so outrageously with Delilah? Melinda yanked out a great clump of bitter cress, wrinkling her nose at its smell. Slade was a swine, a flirt and a degenerate, and she hated him. More bitter cress was flung savagely into the barrow. But gradually the swift, vicious movements of her hands slowed. She stared blindly down at her grubby fingers, hot tears clogging her eyes as she faced the unpalatable truth. Slade was everything she despised, yet she still wanted him.

And her musing must give a new insight to the heroine or the reader, or result in a decision that moves the plot along. Do not show something happening and then have the heroine think it all through again without adding anything to the scene.

Padding

Padding is every sentence, every word that could be cut without affecting the final novel. Padding makes otherwise meek and kind-hearted readers angry: if you use too many details in a minor scene, if you make scenes of unimportant events, if you don't have something happening to further the relationship in every scene, your reader is going to dislike your book. 'Boring,' she'll mutter, tossing it aside. 'Nothing happens. Just two people wittering on and on and getting nowhere.'

So if Slade's secretary is just a bit player, only appearing once or twice, don't spend three paragraphs describing her. Your reader will subconsciously look for her to take some important role later. Those three paragraphs are a blind alley, slowing the pace of your book.

Let your secondary characters do their part to help the plot along, then shoo them off-stage while you get back to the vital business of telling the story of your hero and heroine.

Even main characters can be over-described. If the hero needs three pages to get out of his truck while you describe his personality, his mood, his background, his hopes and dreams and how he feels about the heroine whom he's just caught sight of, then almost all of it is padding.

Surprise

Surprise enhances pace, but give your reader clues and hints, teasing her along with the knowledge that there is more to the story than you've yet revealed. If you fill her in too completely beforehand – especially on something the hero or heroine doesn't know – your climactic scene can fall very flat.

Don't confuse physical action with story action, or think that dramatic events will speed the pace. You may have written a great earthquake scene, but unless it advances the love story it doesn't belong in a romance.

Lazy words

Each word in the manuscript has to be made to count. Any word that isn't doing anything useful has to go.

Watch for sneaky little words and phrases that clog your sentences without doing any work: well, yes, no, very, rather, at all, situated, it was obvious that (and other phrases ending in 'that', or beginning with 'it was' or 'that were'). There are many others you will learn to recognise.

Sometimes you need an extra word or phrase for sentence rhythm, but choose the right one to enhance the sentence in other ways; to complete the picture or add to the mood. Make it specific – 'sizzling' rather than 'hot', or 'blindingly blue' rather than 'brightly coloured'.

Don't repeat information. A crafty and often unconscious way of doing this is to use different words in consecutive sentences or even in the same sentence to say essentially the same thing: 'Gunmetal eyes, steely and hard.'

Another is to have characters telling one another things the reader already knows. This kills pace, because although the writing may be pretty the story is not moving.

Every incident, every careful description or witty comment that doesn't push the plot along, reveal character, or establish setting or mood must be ruthlessly excised. They will ruin your pace and make the focus of your story fuzzy.

Focus

A romance is a story about two people and their emotional reactions to each other, and everything relates to this central focus.

In short category romances this narrowness of vision is an essential ingredient. Some bigger books in which the plot is driven by the love story may have room for more diverse events and characters, but if you set out to write a romance the focus needs to be firmly maintained. For a longer book you may widen it to bring peripheral characters into sharper view, but the hero and heroine must still be at the centre of your mental viewfinder.

Families, friends, jobs and scenery have parts to play *if* they heighten the tension, add to the atmosphere, inform the reader about the characters, or move the plot. But they must not impede the story, which is about Slade and Melinda's romance.

If she's having problems with a hostile takeover of her multimillion dollar business, and it has nothing to do with her romance, you don't have room to mention it, except perhaps in passing.

If he must phone his elderly mother in Zimbabwe every night, mention it because it throws light on his character, but the reader doesn't want to hear all about the old lady's rheumatism or listen in while she tells him to wear his woollies.

Point of view

Many romance readers dislike first person ('I') stories, and some publishers are unwilling to look at them. Until recently most romances were written in the third person (she did this and that) but from the heroine's viewpoint, as if the writer were sitting on her shoulder. Dual viewpoint (the hero's and the heroine's) is increasingly popular, even required by some editors for some lines, although it can be a tricky technique to master. And there have been books and subseries told only from the hero's viewpoint.

You can easily lose pace and focus by swapping between viewpoints, and for beginners sticking firmly to the heroine's point of view is usually best. The reader sees what Melinda sees, what she thinks and what she does, and events where she is not present are normally described to her (and the reader) by someone else.

This is not true reality, it's virtual reality.

At the beginning of a book when you are introducing the viewpoint character to the reader, it sometimes works to use the 'God's eye view' to describe your heroine from an outsider's standpoint. But even here it's seldom wise to give an opinion on her looks. Although the story is told in third person, readers cringe when the narrator (the writer) describes the heroine in glowing, admiring terms ('She had exquisite, petal-like skin; long, fluttering lashes fringed beautiful green eyes'). Use neutral adjectives – pale, tall, dark-haired. You can probably get away with 'emerald-green' but not 'eyes like sparkling emeralds'.

Mention hair and eye colour and other physical character-istics briefly in the first chapter, though not necessarily all at once. There is no requirement for minute descriptions of eye-brows, nose shape and the particular curve of her lips. The reader needs a general idea – she can fill in the finer details from her own imagination, and may well prefer to. And even from your perch on her shoulder you can describe the heroine in ways that don't make her sound vain.

> ...Jacinta opened the car door just a hundred metres from a glorious beach, and unfurled her long, thin body and legs...
>
> A half-smile lifted the corners of her controlled mouth as she unlatched the gate and walked up the white shell path, amused at how pale her narrow feet looked. Ah, well, a few walks along that sweep of sand she'd seen from the hill would soon give them some colour. Although she turned sallow in winter, her skin loved summer, gilding slowly under layers of sunscreen. (*A Forbidden Desire*, Robyn Donald)

Slide into the POV character in the first few pages. After that, stepping outside the narrative encroaches on the reader's private relationship with the story. Authorial comment is an intrusion.

If Melinda's aunt says that although she has her mother's green eyes she is the plainest of her family, or her father remarks that she missed getting her mother's looks, that gives the reader a clue to her appearance as well as to her upbringing and possible hangups about herself.

Or the hero may say that he has no time for long-legged air-headed blondes, which gives you a plot point and an insight into *his* prejudices as well as sneakily describing your heroine for the reader.

Best friends, flatmates or beloved family retainers are notorious for removing the focus from the protagonists and slowing the pace. If you start the book with your heroine talking with a girlfriend, make sure you stay firmly in the heroine's point of view, so that it is clear which woman is the central figure of the story. A confused reader will lose her trust in you.

It is usually not a good idea to get inside a third person's head in a short book. Let them say what they're thinking or convey it by their actions. In a bigger book you may be able to handle multiple viewpoints, but readers find frequent head-hopping disconcerting. Only very skilled writers carry it off successfully. Try to stick to one viewpoint, at least within a scene. When switching to another, clearly signal with a double line space and/or the new viewpoint character's name at the beginning of the paragraph.

Whenever you switch viewpoints or introduce peripheral characters, even in longer books, you risk losing focus and pace. Keep your cast of characters to as few as you really need.

You do want to provide some sort of context for your hero and heroine, who shouldn't appear to live in a vacuum, but other parts of their lives can be sketched lightly.

Send Melinda's witty best friend to Rarotonga, retire the housekeeper, and put the dog in the kennels – unless it's going to drag the hero out from behind a truck so they can meet.

If the heroine's best friend has just lost her mother, we need to know about it only if it affects the plot or reveals that the heroine is a compassionate character with enough loyalty to sit with her friend in her hour of need rather than go out dancing.

Slade's thoughts should be centred on Melinda. A romance is not about his work or his sport or his mates. It is about the woman in his life. For the purposes of this book she is all that matters in his world. You are writing about their love, not their work, their family, their place in society – or life, the universe and everything.

If the hero is not present the conversation had better be about him, or the heroine doing something that will affect him.

Keeping this focus also helps to maintain that vital ingredient, emotional intensity (see Emotional Impact, p. 76).

Whenever something important to the development of their relationship happens, write a scene so that the reader is there.

Romance heroines and heroes often have no living family and few visible friends. This has to do with the mythical tradition in romance, with archetypes, and with the theory of human development, but these are all subliminal. (If you are interested in this aspect of romantic mythology and the reasons other than pure escapism for the popularity of romance, read *The Secular Scripture* and other works of Northrop Frye, *The Hero with a Thousand Faces* and *The Power of Myth* by Joseph Campbell, and *Dangerous Men and Adventurous Women* edited by Jayne Ann Krentz.) On a practical level, writers know they have a limited number of pages and can't clutter up the narrative with a lot of extraneous characters.

Every one of your 55,000–100,000 words must tell the reader either directly or obliquely about the progress of the romance.

If minor characters run away with the book, or seem more interesting than the main characters, or if you feel stifled by this tight focus, perhaps you are trying to write the wrong kind of book for your interests, and should look for a genre or subgenre that allows more scope. Family or historical sagas, glitz and glamour books, and mainstream 'women's fiction' can accommodate longer and less tautly written stories that deal with other matters than the love life of two people.

After the resolution give the reader time to absorb everything that has happened, without allowing the conclusion to meander on after everything that needs to be said has been said. A lyrical, romantic and flowing passage may be just what you need here to close the story, but keep it short – as a general rule, no more than a paragraph.

6. Setting

Readers need to know where in the world they are, so indicate or at least hint at geographical location and immediate background early on in the book – before the reader forms an erroneous view that will be rudely jolted at some stage.

Location

If the reader assumes the book is taking place in rural England, and nothing suggests otherwise until Chapter Five when the heroine drives to Alice Springs in the heart of Australia, you have hurled your reader right out of the world of the book and into cold, hard reality.

If your location or setting is very unusual (the Antarctic, an oil rig) the average reader will have fewer reference points stored in her memory to complete the picture. So more detail is appropriate.

Romances attract a world-wide audience. You may need to explain any purely local objects or national customs. Unless your point-of-view character is new to the country, describe these things from the viewpoint of someone who is accustomed to them. You are writing a story, not a disguised textbook or travelogue.

A skilled writer can make any place exciting and intriguing with the right descriptive touch and appropriate characters. By all means take note of the oft-repeated advice to write about what you know – but don't let that limit you.

If you want to set your novel in Fiji it helps if you've lived there, but if you haven't, talk to people who've been there, interview Fijians, read good travel books about Fiji, watch videos about it, listen to Fijian music, and research Fiji on the Internet if you're a Net-surfer. And then get somebody who knows Fiji to read the completed manuscript so they can tell you whether you've made any mistakes. You owe it to your reader not to insult her with sloppy research.

Or you can make up your own island, as both Robyn and Daphne have done. Again, this has to be in keeping – that is, Fala'isi had to be recognisably a Pacific island, with the correct flora and fauna and physical features.

You are inviting the reader into a world you have created, but it must be rooted as firmly as it can be in reality. If something grates it jerks the reader out of your imaginary world and back, with a thud, into her own.

Writers do invent places, but we would not put a large city in what we know is a predominantly rural area, nor a ten thousand acre sheep station on the outskirts of our largest city.

Although the location must seem authentic, Robyn doesn't dwell on the fact that New Zealand's Northland mosquitoes tend to eat her after dark. Romance doesn't need mosquitoes, unless the heroine's allergy to them necessitates her staying in the hero's house.

Setting

Settings can be geographical, architectural, occupational, historical. A city or a village, an igloo or an opera house, a forest hut or yacht or high-rise office building may be the main setting for your story. Make it seem real without overwhelming the reader with irrelevant description. Pick two or three details of vegetation, scenery, furnishings or fittings to give a brief sketch. A little description goes a very long way.

Books should be set in a vividly realised place, but make judicious and sparing use of local colour. A few carefully chosen details give an impressionistic picture of the setting.

Smell, sight and hearing are all important. Try for the exact phrase that gives a sense of place.

> When she opened her side door just after sunrise, haunting organ notes reached into the fresh saltiness of the morning, drawing her gaze down and along the gully to the old house, its empty windows burnished to flax-flower orange by the morning sun. (*Summer Seduction*, Daphne Clair)

Don't tell. Show! And don't do both:

> White leather sofas faced each other stiffly across a gleaming parquet floor. Melinda watched as Slade pulled silk tweed curtains to hide the waterfront view below the penthouse. Spotlit Picassos glowed on the wall. Heavens, Melinda thought, Slade must be extremely rich. And he obviously likes modern furniture and art too.

The last two sentences are unnecessary.

Every scene or description is an integral part of the story, pushing the plot along and revealing character. Something should be happening in the scenery.

The details you choose should emphasise – or contrast with – the mood of the scene.

Relate setting and scene to tone and mood, and use them whenever possible to further the plot. Local geography and weather patterns can bring in plot elements. Bush fires, floods or accidents at sea might be useful for precipitating climaxes or mini-climaxes. In a romance, however, *outside events are not the climax* of the story, because the story is about emotions. The real climax is an emotional storm within – or between – the hero and heroine.

Some settings are so closely allied to the story that they are virtually a character or the source of the tension. In Gothic romances houses that exude menace or mystery are a necessary ingredient of the genre. Unusual settings are more likely to assume this degree of importance, and indeed there is no point in using a very unusual background unless it has direct relevance to the story and is fully integrated into it.

Use verbs a lot in describing settings. Even houses can huddle, brood, squat or rear. Be sparing and particular with adjectives, seldom using more than one before a noun. For the most part choose the words you use in normal conversation, perhaps with a slightly heightened awareness if that suits the story, a little more formality, and a judicious occasional use of an unusual word that has the precise meaning you want to convey or that enhances sentence rhythm. If it's the one right word, that's the word you use.

Many budding romance writers are excellent at descriptions of landscape. But don't let the beauty of the location and your lovingly crafted descriptions interfere with the movement of the plot towards its resolution. Use people – even anonymous people – to breathe life into scenery.

The next day about a hundred islanders turned up on the beach front to build temporary homes for the visitors. Groups of women picnicked on the white sand under the palms, criticising the work in progress, and children and a number of pigs scampered about unhindered among the dozens of workers, splashing in and out of the clear, rippling lagoon. But by the end of the day the men had erected, amid much laughter and singing, a small hut for Melinda, a larger one for Slade, and a long low sleeping hut for the other men.

Local colour has to be relevant to the romance. Otherwise it has no purpose.

If your heroine is with the hero at the dragon boat races, scatter the bits of description along the path of the story, and be sure that attending the event advances your plot. Don't abandon or ignore plot and characters.

Readers enjoy Robyn's descriptions of gardens but they are there for a reason. In *A Matter of Will* the hero, Matt, takes the heroine to see a thrush's nest in his garden. This was to show that despite growing up in a beautiful place he didn't take it for granted; and because he was rather aloof the scene also revealed his softer side.

The historical romance

Historical romance is published in both category and single title formats (see pp. 10 and 11).

A reader picking up a book labelled 'historical romance' expects a wonderful love story set in a former time and perhaps a different place. Because she may be unfamiliar with the period, she needs a much more detailed evocation of setting.

Historical writers need considerable skill to convey all the necessary information about their setting without hitting the reader over the head with long expositional paragraphs. They have to discipline themselves not to throw in every fascinating fact they uncover in their research. And without authorial intrusion they must describe everyday things familiar to the characters but not the reader.

It is not sufficient to dress up modern characters in period costumes, surround them with historical trappings and give them quaint dialogue. The writer needs to know the *attitudes* of the time in order to draw convincing historical characters and build plots that could only belong in that setting.

Medieval women were often resourceful and knowledgeable – but were subject to arranged dynastic marriages. Nice Georgian girls didn't venture into the streets alone, yet dressed skimpily to show off their breasts and legs. A Victorian man whose bride was not a virgin was entitled to be outraged – even if he himself had seduced her! Well into this century a girl's reputation and probably her life was ruined if she spent a night, however innocently or accidentally, with a man, and a decent man would have married her forthwith.

Any of these could be the starting point for a historical romance.

Remember, romance is about courtship. Regency romances in the tradition of Georgette Heyer are particularly noted for historical details appropriate to courtship rituals.

Preening is a courtship ritual, so clothing and hairstyle assume importance. Dancing is a courtship ritual much used in historical romance. Food is often mentioned. Remember the scene in *Tom Jones* where eating became symbolic fore-play? Even the proper Victorians thought chocolates were an acceptable gift from a man to a woman.

Many historical romances dwell on details of dress, food and social events rather than politics, battles and social evils.

They may touch lightly on the plight of the sweeper's boy or the pregnant maidservant, and the main characters may well have a social conscience and even a reformer's zeal.

Important political or social questions, battles and historic events may be vital to character or plot development but they are not the story.

The story is about the hero and the heroine and how they come to know, love and almost certainly marry each other. Everything else in a romance is there to serve this central plot. But all those details of dress, speech, etc. must be accurate. Many of the readers are very knowledgeable about their favourite period in history.

The children's library is a good place to start finding basic information. Look also for writings of the time, social histories, books on costume and on antique furniture, and the journals of historical societies. Study bibliographies for more leads.

The line between a historical romance and a historical novel with a strong romance subplot sometimes blurs. *Gone With the Wind* is usually labelled 'romance' but the story of Scarlett's determination to save her heritage could well stand without the relationship between her and Rhett Butler. It would not, of course, be the same book. And would probably not have been a best-seller.

A strong romantic thread is an asset to a historical novel, and the best of them inextricably intertwine romance and history.

Some historical series successsfully blend action and romance; they involve the characters in more than one roman-tic enounter along the way but ultimately bring one couple together. Two examples are the Lymond and the Niccolo series by Dorothy Dunnett, and the Jamie/Claire series (*Cross Stitch*, *Voyager*, etc.) by Diana Gabaldon.

In any fiction, the story is the important thing, and it should never be clouded by extraneous descriptive passages. If they don't enhance the story mood, plot or characterisation they have no place in the book.

7. The Language of Love

There is no special language for romantic novels. The core of a romance is the emotion rather than the language. Top-selling writers vary from those whose style is spare and simple and nearly transparent, to those who glory in extravagant language and images. There are many ways to convey the warmth and excitement that romance readers look for.

Lovers experience the world through heightened senses, so romance writing involves touch and sight, sound and hearing and scent, evoking the infinite variety of sensuous experiences.

We write about emotions, and writers and readers need not be embarrassed at that.

Romance has been criticised for a lack of originality in language. One of the pleasures of romantic novels is that they are to some extent written in a shared language which regular readers understand, in the same way that avid science-fiction readers enjoy a particular techno-jargon common to that genre, which writers borrow fairly freely from each other.

These code words and phrases – a kind of romance writers' and readers' shorthand – are difficult to avoid because of the baggage they carry with them (the muscle in his jaw, the pulse in her throat). Some words – like 'mocking' and 'sardonic' – have acquired a particular meaning in the genre, signalling certain emotions and character reactions. Experienced readers relate to them on a deep, intuitive level.

A few well-understood code phrases used where they are doing a useful job will hardly be noticed. But a narrative consisting almost entirely of these looks unoriginal and stale.

It is *not* all right to string a lot of well-used ideas and phrases together and call them a book. Romantic writers of the fifties and sixties invented many of the expressions and images we now know so well. Nineties writers need to create new ones.

There are only so many words in the language. It's the way you arrange them that matters.

Write in your own style and voice. Never try to 'write like' any other author, or 'like a romance novel'. What is wanted is an original voice telling an age-old story in a fresh, new way.

Editors have their own pet hates – words and phrases they never want to see again. You should have read enough in the genre to be able to identify the most overused clichés and avoid them whenever possible. As a reminder, watch out for the overused phrases listed below.

Try to come up with new images, but there is a danger in trying so hard that you become precious or pretentious. You don't want your manuscript to read as though your thesaurus wrote it. And don't invent words. They seldom work and will stop the reader in her tracks.

Clichés
a raised eyebrow (singular)
a sardonic smile
arms of steel (or steely arms)
burgeoning breasts (hers)
every fibre of her being
hair-roughened chest (his)
he gritted
he husked (don't!)
he plundered her lips
he said thickly
her silken core
her silken anything!
her traitorous lips/heart/body
his greedy kisses/mouth
his manhood (especially when rising)
his mocking laughter

his sculpted features
plundered the honeyed sweetness within (her mouth or any-
where else...)
she knew no more
shell-like ears
taut thighs (his)
the muscle in his jaw
the pulse in his/her throat
the secret places of her body
the strong column of his neck
etc. etc. etc.

'Disembodied' eyes

There is a purist school that sternly disapproves of the word
'eyes' in place of 'gaze'. Careless use of literary convention
can certainly produce ludicrous prose: 'She dropped her eyes
to the tomatoes and ate them.' 'His eyes darted about the
room and then ran over her.' 'She had her eye on the chair
before he sat on it.'

But 'gaze' is an intrusive word because the letter 'z' tends to
catch the reader's eye, and several in a paragraph is too many.
It has long been accepted that in literature eyes wander, meet,
lower and even on occasion fly, as in 'her eyes flew to his face'.
The use of metaphor is part of the writer's toolkit. We suggest
you use 'eyes' carefully but don't get hung up about it.

Dialogue

People develop relationships, learn about each other and
deepen their understanding through talking. What they talk
about and how they talk is very important to the development
of their love story. Women complain that real-life men don't
talk to them; the romance hero talks! (Even in bed – or especially in bed!)

Slade tells Melinda she's beautiful, he flirts with her, he argues with her – he doesn't slam off into another room, or sulk.

Mastering the art of writing good dialogue is essential. Dialogue looks interesting and inviting on the page, and starting a book or chapter with snappy dialogue is a good hook. Most people find other people's overheard conversations fascinating.

Real dialogue meanders; it has great gaping holes, people talk over each other and interrupt and don't finish sentences. If you wrote it down word for word it would be dull and hard to follow. What you have to do is produce dialogue that reads realistically, while cutting out all the ums and ahs and non sequiturs of real speech.

Written dialogue won't be the same as real conversation, it'll just seem real.

In fiction people don't bother with unimportant conversations. Even a conversation about the weather must have some bearing on the progress of the relationship. A banal conversation may counterpoint the internal turmoil of the characters or point up their unease with each other, or it may contain subtext – what they are really saying to each other underneath the conventional words.

'It's suddenly become very chilly in here,' can mean, 'The heating has gone on the blink,' or 'I realise that you're giving me the cold shoulder.' If the first, it doesn't belong unless it means that Slade and Melinda will have to huddle under one blanket all night to keep from freezing, thus furthering their relationship. (We have more to say about subtext at the end of this chapter.)

Dialogue should not repeat what the reader has already seen. Do not have a character go off to tell another all that has happened in a previous scene, unless it is important for the plot. Carry on from *after* that part of the conversation or simply leave out what the reader has seen and concentrate on the listener's reaction.

Perhaps, she thought, half hopefully, she had judged him somewhat severely.

[Chapter break]

'Rubbish,' Pandora said. 'It's the old male chauvinist owner-ship thing, that's all. Poaching on another man's property and all that.'

Pandora was always a very satisfying listener, and tonight she was true to form, shrieking with laughter when Alexia explained how the interview had been conducted at cross-purposes.

'You said that to his *face*?' she squealed... 'If it had been me I'd have walloped him with my handbag for good measure.'

'Well, I gave him his comeuppance far more subtly and with just as much effect as felling him with my handbag.'

'How?'

'I wrote up the interview the next day. It wasn't kind.'

(Abridged from *The Rainbow Way* by Laurey Bright)

Good dialogue sparkles and has rhythm, and witty dialogue is wonderful if you can do it.

A character using several short, staccato sentences in succession helps indicate to the reader that he is nervous or under stress, or simply that this person is not very articulate.

Use words and speech patterns that occur in normal speech, but slightly enhanced. In moments of high emotion characters may use language and say things that people would not often say in real life, but they don't use poetic words and images and talk like Victorian lovers throughout the book unless the author has established that they are people who habitually do so.

In dialogue one person doesn't usually rabbit on at length. They almost always speak in short snatches, not more than two or three sentences at a time.

Use contractions (don't, can't, won't) in dialogue, because that's how people speak.

If you have a character with an accent or who speaks in a dialect, use the rhythm of that type of speech, rather than trying to reproduce it exactly. One or two foreign words or a particular sentence structure will tag the character. Trying to faithfully reproduce a dialect too often stops the reader reading while she tries to work out what all those strange words peppered with apostrophes actually mean.

In historical novels don't lard the dialogue too heavily with 'Zounds!' and 'La' – a little of that goes a very long way. Certainly use colourful language of the time, but it's usually best to keep most of this for minor characters, and have your main characters speak more formally than we do, with fewer contractions but naturally.

When a character answers a question, leaving out the initial 'Yes' or 'No' – unless that's all they say – and just using the rest of the answer speeds up the pace.

Like everything else, dialogue should further the plot and reveal something about the character who is speaking. And if it contains subtext, go to the top of the class.

Using dialogue to convey information to the reader is a two-edged sword. It can be a useful technique, but beware.

> Melinda turned to her sister, saying impetuously, 'How I wish George Deere, our father, the millionaire, and his fifth wife Freda whom I despise but you're always smarming up to, would get here before 7 o'clock this tenth night of August 1791. Here in Moonshott Manor in Cornwall it's always dark by 6 o'clock and I fret so about them driving in their coach and four across the moors to our cliffside home, although I know you don't give a hoot.'

Don't do it that way!

Always be suspicious when you have a character telling another something they both know already. A danger signal is having one character say to another, 'As you know...'

Information can be conveyed by dialogue skilfully and in brief:

♥ 'Is it true what they say about blondes?'

♥ 'I know you could buy and sell this firm.'

♥ 'I thought you were in Australia. What are you doing back in Auckland?'

♥ 'You hardly know me! It's barely three weeks since we met.'

♥ 'At eighteen I didn't know any better.'

One way to use dialogue to convey information known to both speakers is to have one fling it at the other – as people do in real life when quarrelling:

> 'If you hadn't walked out on me without so much as a goodbye, I wouldn't have married Marmaduke!'
>
> 'I was kidnapped by Martians! You ought to have known I'd never leave you willingly. But oh, no – you couldn't wait for ten minutes to hook the richest man you could find.'
>
> 'Ten minutes? It was ten years!'
>
> 'You're lying! It can't have been more than ten days at the most.'
>
> 'How stupid do you think I am, Slade? That story might do for one of your TV scripts, but try it on the studio, not me!'
>
> 'There was a time when you'd have believed anything I told you, Melinda.'
>
> 'Yes, and look what that got me! Do you have any idea what it's like to be a solo mother? I'll always be grateful to Marmaduke for saving me from that.'
>
> 'He's a hundred years old!' Slade said, his lip curling with distaste.
>
> 'He's fifty-five,' Melinda answered coldly. 'You always were prone to exaggeration. You couldn't even give me one child like any normal man,' she added bitterly. 'It had to be triplets!'

Use dialogue to reveal the push/pull effect of sexual tension, the conflict, and the characters of both protagonists. Contrast dialogue with the small, betraying movements – action cues –

that reveal the speaker's emotions. And remember, men and women speak differently.

Men tend to make flat, abbreviated statements, whereas women are more verbal and often ask for agreement.

♥ 'It's cold,' Slade said.

♥ 'Isn't it cold today?' Melinda said.

Men and women use different vocabularies too:

♥ 'She's utterly adorable,' Melinda breathed.

♥ 'A great kid,' Slade agreed.

Listen to the men and women in your life.

Dialogue should reflect the background, personality and emotions of the speaker. If the hero is self-confident and knows he is attractive to women this should show in his behaviour and dialogue – although you don't want him to seem conceited or smug.

Theoretically you should be able to distinguish each character by their words alone. This is a counsel of perfection but it is something to strive for.

Leave out of dialogue

♥ Repetitive phrases or sentences – unless they're being used to 'tag' a minor character.

♥ Clichés – ditto.

♥ Slang expressions that will date your work.

♥ Speech tags that don't give any further information than the dialogue itself. ('Go to hell!' he said angrily. 'I can't bear it!' she cried in anguish.)

♥ Greetings, leavetakings, and the normal trivial enquiries about the health of the other party or the other party's relatives, pets, etc. (Though a seemingly innocuous query like 'And how is Delilah?' may be a loaded question, meaning, 'I know you've been seeing that conniving bitch behind my back!') which brings us to –

Subtext

Subtext is what's happening behind what's on the page. It is the real story, the emotion behind the words – the hidden meaning that the reader infers from what the writer implies.

Subtext is that which is not directly stated – what the writer knows about her characters but does not tell, and what the reader will believe because she has not been told it. Used well, it increases emotional impact (see pp. 76–83).

When you describe your heroine picking up and comforting a hurt child, the subtext is that this is a kindhearted woman. When she calmly disinfects and bandages the wound you do not need to inform your reader that this is also a sensible woman. When she hands over the child to its mother and has to turn away to hide a tear, the subtext is that she is emotionally affected by the incident, the child, or children in general. The reader may know, or find out later, that she has lost or longs for a child of her own.

The text describes actions and words; the subtext implies the emotions and character underlying them.

Subtext is particularly important in dialogue.

If the protagonists always say exactly what they mean the dialogue can be flat, predictable and uninteresting. It is the subtext that makes dialogue sizzle, when the meaning underneath what the characters are saying is much more important than the words they use.

Sarcasm is the most obvious form of subtext – where what you say is exactly the opposite of what you mean. Usually there is no mistaking the real message. But sometimes, rather than being obvious, subtext is oblique.

A subtle subtext may be conveyed partly by dialogue,

partly in narrative, and particularly by action cues and body language – as in Daphne's *The Wayward Bride*.

Pierce is having a drink at Trista's home while they wait for her father. He has taken her out just once some weeks ago and has not asked again.

> 'Dad says you have a tricky case coming up.' She took a sip of her sherry.
> 'Yes. I've been pretty busy preparing for it.'
> She looked up briefly, then took another quick sip. 'How busy?'
> He hesitated, then said quite gently, 'Not that busy.'

On the surface the conversation is a simple social interchange.

But what is really happening? Trista is asking Pierce why he has not taken her out again. She hopes it is simply because he's not had time for a social life lately. He tries to avoid a direct rebuff by agreeing that yes, he's been very busy. But Trista wants to clarify the issue and she backs him into a corner. At the same time her body language shows that she is not as bold or as confident as she would like.

Pierce refuses to be pressured. He thinks before he speaks – hesitates – and because he is not a man to be manipulated, yet doesn't wish to hurt or humiliate her, he is firm but kind – making it clear he has no intention of asking her out again, but without using the brutal words 'I don't want to.'

Subtext is useful when characters are verbally sparring.

> He said, 'You can cheer me on... and cheer me up if we lose.'
> 'What if you win?'
> 'Ah! Then I expect the usual winner's perks.'
> 'I didn't know I was supposed to bring a laurel wreath.'
> 'It wasn't a laurel wreath I was thinking of.' His gaze slipped to her mouth briefly before he returned his attention to the road. (*Grounds For Marriage*, Daphne Clair)

It's more fun and more civilised to exchange hidden meanings in public than come right out and say 'I want to go to bed with you,' and 'I think I might like that, but I'm not settling for mere sex.' In the above example there are two children in the car with the adult characters, so the sexual undertone in the conversation must be kept oblique.

Sometimes the subtext of a scene does not become obvious until another scene has taken place later in the book. The clues are all there, but not apparent until further on in the story, so readers will refer back in their minds to earlier scenes. This gives a nice density to a book, and guards against readers feeling cheated by sudden revelations for which the writer has failed to lay any groundwork (see 'plot devices', pp. 35–36).

If dialogue seems flat and uninteresting, see if you can liven it up with subtext. Even if the reader isn't exactly sure why, she will usually sense that there is more to this exchange than meets the eye. (The excerpt below from *Reckless Engagement* shows how the scene was as Daphne first wrote it, and then after she teased out the scene's subtext.)

Don't get too carried away with your own cleverness, though. There's a fine line between intriguing and baffling. It can irritate readers if they don't know what the hell is going on!

Subtext adds texture, meaning and interest to your book and knowing how to write it is one of the greatest assets of a romance writer. Good romances are filled with it, because readers really enjoy discovering the hidden meanings behind the words on the page.

Subtext in use

This example well illustrates what a difference subtext makes.

Read this scene where Katrien and Zachary go climbing:

'Okay, we can rest here for a while.'

He wiped his face with a gloved hand, staring out at the surrounding countryside – bleak and brown near the mountain, mistily green further away.

Katrien subsided on the snow. 'And you do this for fun?'
'You're not enjoying it?'

She gazed about them and admitted, 'The view is pretty spectacular.'

'Worth it?'

But she wasn't ready to concede that. 'How far are we going?' She squinted at the forbidding wall of rock – in some places too steep to hold the snow – that loomed above them.

'How far do you want to go?'

'We couldn't make it to the top in the time we've got, could we?'

'No,' he agreed. 'Not if you don't feel ready for it.'

When she began to get cold she pushed herself to her feet. 'All right, MacDuff,' she sighed. 'Let's move on.'

'You're game?' He glanced at the unwelcoming terrain above them.

'If you are,' she agreed.

'Remember what I told you. Let me know if you're in trouble.'

It was all right at first... but... the snow suddenly seemed to disappear under her boots... and she found herself dangling in space, witless with terror.

...With his help she was able to crawl back onto the snow-covered slope. He held the rope firm, reefing it in as she panted towards him.

She collapsed into his arms, her breath coming in shuddering gasps. 'An easy beginners' climb, you said!'

'You're okay. I've got you.'

Here is the same scene with subtext added:

'Okay, we can rest here for a while.'

There was sweat on his forehead too, although he wasn't flushed with exertion like her. The cold air seemed to have bleached the outdoor tan from his cheeks. He wiped his face with a gloved hand, staring out at the surrounding countryside – bleak and brown near the mountain, mistily green further away.

Katrien subsided on the snow. 'And you do this for fun?'

He glanced down at her and laughed shortly. 'You're not enjoying it?'

She gazed about them and admitted, 'The view is pretty spectacular.'

'Worth it?'

But she wasn't ready to concede that. 'How far are we going?' She squinted at the forbidding wall of rock – in some places too steep to hold the snow – that loomed above them.

He didn't answer immediately, but stood up and she turned to look at him, shading her eyes because the sun lay behind him, making his features dark and indistinguishable. Her heart thumped once with a quick, irrational, complicated emotion, a stirring of familiarity.

'How far,' he asked her, 'do you want to go?'

'Not all the way,' she answered. Then quickly added, 'We couldn't make it to the summit in the time we've got, could we?'

'No,' he agreed, after a tiny pause. 'Not if you don't feel ready for it.'

When she began to get cold she pushed herself to her feet. 'All right, MacDuff,' she sighed. 'Let's move on.'

'You're game?' He glanced at the unwelcoming terrain above them.

'If you are,' she agreed lightly.

He gave her an oddly searching look, then a faint smile. 'Remember what I told you. Let me know if you're in trouble.'

It was all right at first, hard work but not difficult... but the snow suddenly seemed to disappear under her boots...

She slid over a hidden overhang and found herself dangling in space, witless with terror. But... with his help was able to crawl back onto the snow-covered slope. He held the rope firm, reefing it in as she panted towards him.

She collapsed into his arms, her breath coming in shuddering gasps. 'An easy beginners' climb, you said!'

'You're okay.' His breath feathered her ear as his arms tightened round her. 'It's all right, I'm not going to let you go.' (Adapted from *Reckless Engagement* by Daphne Clair)

8. Emotional Impact

Emotional impact (also called emotional punch or emotional intensity) is the heart of romance. It can make the difference between acceptance and rejection. If there is a 'secret' to romance writing, this is it.

Emotional impact is what readers want from a romance, the basic appeal of the entire genre, the one thing that makes romances different from any other kind of book. It is what editors look for and hope to find in every manuscript they read. If a writer cannot deliver this necessary element the book will fail as a romance, just as a cake with all the right ingredients except a raising agent will emerge from the baking flat and heavy and indigestible.

There are writers whose technical skills may not stand up to stringent literary criticism but who are instinctively able to deliver this magical experience. This is why you will occasionally see books that 'are not nearly as well-written as mine' on the shelves when your carefully crafted manuscript has been sent back with a polite letter.

While some romances are 'throbbers' all the way through, keeping the characters and the reader in a state of high tension from start to finish, others are softer or lighter, with the tension subtle and low-key during most of the book. But the promise of all romances is to give the reader an emotionally intense experience.

Emotional intensity

Emotional intensity is generated by the source of tension between the characters. A fierce sexual attraction is not the same as emotional intensity. For real tension there must be a cogent reason not to act on the attraction.

Many readers thoroughly enjoy a book in which sparks fly throughout and the protagonists are as liable to quarrel as to kiss, but in some love stories the characters don't argue with each other at all.

It is extraordinarily difficult to produce this gentler kind of book while still providing that vital sense of anticipation that makes the reader want to know what happens next. Very good writers do it without falling into the trap of sentimentality – or worse, boring the reader.

The idea that all romance is founded on misunderstanding and strife between the lovers is wrong. The conflict that produces the tension between them may be entirely in one character's psyche.

Very successful romances have been founded on warmth, wit and style. Above all, style! But there must still be a source of tension, some fundamental suspense in the story, some uncertainty about when and how the resolution and the positive, forward-looking ending will occur. Even the quietest stories usually have a crisis point where the tension is pulled tighter.

A romantic novel must have emotion, because the emotional life of two people at the point of their falling in love is what romance is about. Without emotion between the characters, however subtly expressed, you do not have a romance, any more than you can have a murder mystery without a body lurking somewhere, or a traditional western without a horse and six-gun.

Intense emotion needs a strong *source of tension* (see pp. 28–32) – something more than simply 'sexual tension' which is only one component of it.

In romance, what the writer must convey is emotional

excitement – a different thing from physical arousal. In some books this emotional tension reaches nail-biting intensity.

Emotional intensity is caused by frustration. Often it is the frustration of falling in love with someone who appears to be indifferent or unsuitable or even antagonistic. It is definitely the frustration of falling in love when it is emotionally dangerous – for whatever good reason the writer comes up with – to the protagonists. Whatever happens their lives will never be the same again, and they realise this. They can see that what lies ahead is either intense happiness or intense misery. And they are afraid it will all end in tears.

Emotional punch is intensified by the thwarted desire of your hero and heroine to go to bed together. Or by the fact that going to bed has only made their problems worse.

Intensity of feeling is conveyed mainly by action and especially by dialogue, rather than by exposition or narrative. And it is based on character and motivation.

Dialogue and incidents should reveal the state of the hero and heroine's emotions as well as propelling the story forward.

Scattering 'romantic' words or phrases through a banal storyline with stereotyped characters is not going to produce that special spark. But the romantic intensity is heightened by the right words used in the right way (see Language, p. 62).

Background details (sights, sounds, and especially aromas and textures), precise depictions of body language, and action cues are useful devices.

The writer imagines the scene minutely, richly. The hero's voice may be casual, but are his hands white-knuckled on the steering wheel? Is there a scent of jasmine on the night air as the protagonists touch? Can she feel the body-warmed silk of his shirt against her cheek? Does the sound of the sea counterpoint their lovemaking?

Emotional impact is heightened when the couple are desperately aware of each other and want to have and to hold the other person forever, but one or both sees an insurmountable obstacle in their path and fights the attraction with every breath.

It is heightened when the hero is an emotional threat to the heroine – not a physical threat, although in some plots she may erroneously believe he is, but a threat to her peace of mind, to her image of herself, to the life she has made for herself. So he is dangerous, but eminently desirable. She knows she should turn and run. Unfortunately, for some cogent and believable reason, she can't. So she comes out fighting.

In her turn the heroine can be a definite emotional threat to the hero, for whatever reason you and he decide on: he is happy with his life and he doesn't need a grand passion to complete it; or she is trying to marry his vulnerable half-brother and he believes her to be a liar and a thief.

You need to know – or come to know – your protagonists really well, so that the reason they see each other as a threat fits in with each character and personality, and with what has happened to them in the past.

Romance is about courtship, about foreplay – even if the couple is married (it is then about rediscovering those early feelings they enjoyed when they first met).

The reader wants to feel vicariously the delicious uncertainty and anticipation of the process of falling in love.

Emotional intensity is not sex; it is not loving descriptions of biceps, boobs or other parts of the anatomy, nor of seductive clothing. Nor is it a detailed, clinical description of lovemaking. While emotional intensity must be present in love scenes, consummated sex tends to slacken tension. In fact consummation can ruin tension and dull the emotional impact.

So here you have two people powerfully attracted to each other, yet for some reason they can't afford to give in to that attraction.

What stops them?

The source of tension in your plot is what prevents them from taking that shaky, uncertain step into trusting the person they're learning to love, or, if they do give their trust, ensures they're not allowed to enjoy that luxury for long.

Showing emotional intensity

Concentrate on the tension between the hero and heroine, and their reactions to each other. Sexual awareness should always be smouldering beneath the surface.

This unresolved attraction is the source of emotional intensity – though if the sexual attraction is too overt it often ruins the tension.

These two people don't want to show any vulnerability. Yet they give themselves away all the time – if not to each other, then to the reader.

Contrast what is being said and done with what is being thought and felt:

> Aura fluttered her lashes and cooed, 'How fascinating. Is [your work] dangerous, too?'
>
> 'Sometimes,' Flint said, the intriguing gravelly texture of his voice intensifying. 'Does danger excite you?' From beneath half-closed eyelids he was watching the way the light shimmered across her hair. (*Dark Fire* by Robyn Donald)

The word 'cooed' clues the reader in; heroines do not coo. Aura is being provocative because she is very aware of Flint – as he is of her. His question is a taunt.

Contrast the action with the reaction; show the heroine reacting to the hero. What appeals to her about him? Eyes, hair, build, height, colouring, voice, the way he moves – how do they affect her?

The heroine can hate him or despise him, but she can't be repelled by him. She has to want him – and the reader has to know this, even if the heroine and the hero don't admit it!

Let the reader know how her behaviour, her actions, her physical attributes affect the hero – show, don't tell.

If he has no discernible emotion on his face yet his strong fingers snap a pencil in half we know something rather violent is going on behind that façade.

Even if you are writing in the heroine's point of view you must indicate the hero's feelings by the way he speaks, and by the small physical signs he can't control – body language, tone of voice, eye contact.

It's a language women know well, so use it – preferably without clichés.

Use your own experience. Heighten it a little; but although we are writing fantasy, it's fantasy firmly rooted in reality, so don't have your heroine swooning with ecstasy all the time. She is a sensible woman, even in love.

Emotional impact does not mean overblown writing full of 'romantic' words. It can be conveyed in everyday language. Read different writers, those you feel have this excitement and intensity in their writing. How do they do it?

Maybe their dialogue throbs with subtext (see p. 75) – what the characters say sounds innocuous but what they mean is obviously something much deeper. Maybe the description of the scenery or the setting is so sensuously written that it sets a mood of heightened awareness.

Maybe the minutiae of the way the couple appear to each other, or the way they affect each other, is so carefully delineated that the reader must share their emotion. (Is her skin hot, her limbs oddly fluid? Does the hair on her nape prickle when he comes near? When he looks at her are his eyes more intensely blue?)

You can graft learned techniques onto your own individual voice without slavish copying.

Emotional intensity is lost when

♥ Slade and Melinda fall into each other's arms and consummate their relationship with tenderness and perfect understanding in the first, third or penultimate chapter, and nothing happens after that except a deepening relationship.

♥ There is nothing to keep them from falling into each other's arms and living happily ever after except a series of coincidences, random happenings or foolish misunderstandings.

♥ The reasons they don't fall into each other's... etc. are trite, trivial, unconvincing.

♥ The author keeps explaining why they're not falling into each other's... etc. by playing ping-pong inside their heads, and relaying every hope, uncertainty and doubt to the reader.

'Head-hopping' is extremely difficult to do well. Beginners are advised to practise the single POV first, although some markets do prefer dual POV, and if you want to write for them you will need to learn how to do it skilfully (see Point of view on pp. 51–54).

Love scenes

Love scenes are as much a part of the plot as any other scene. If a love scene is the next logical step in the plot, it should happen.

It should be at least mildly erotic, but neither clinical nor twee. The degree of description is a matter of the writer's taste, discretion and skill, and the particular demands of the story. What happens 'in bed' (or at the beach or under the waterfall or on the grand piano) – and how – should be crucial to plot and to the revelation or development of character.

A love scene – like any other scene – must further complicate the issue that keeps the lovers apart. Rather than resolving the tension, it should create more problems (unless it's the resolution itself and takes place in the last chapter). Or it may be the perfect opportunity to combine thought or discussion with physical action.

Don't let the lovers get as far as the sheets and then be stopped by a knock on the door, telephone call, fire, flood, or asteroid impact. Ask yourself what you're trying to show in the scene. If it's just that they want each other, there are less clichéd ways of doing it.

And remember, their sexual compatibility is not likely to be the central issue; there are other, vitally important things at stake – trust, commitment, understanding.

Conclusion

We soul-searched a great deal about this subject in order to teach our students 'how to do it'. At times we wondered if that elusive 'emotional punch' or emotional intensity was something in the genes of certain writers. We came to a conclusion at last that emotional impact, as we finally decided to call it, happens when everything else works perfectly.

9. Dear Editor: Query Letters, Synopses and Proposals

In the past, publishers routinely accepted unsolicited manuscripts (i.e. manuscripts sent to them without prior contact). Increasingly, publishers insist that new writers must send a query letter, a synopsis or a proposal before they will consider a manuscript (also called ms).

A *query letter* asks an editor at a publishing house whether she'd be interested in seeing your manuscript. Consult one of the available reference books (see pp. 89–90) to make sure that this particular house publishes the sort of book you plan to write. It's no use sending a historical romance of 100,000 words – however brilliant it is – to a publisher that publishes contemporary novels of no longer than 55,000 words. Many romance publishers send guidelines on request to help writers meet their requirements.

When your book is almost finished, address your query letter to a specific editor, unless the guidelines say not to. The editor you see listed in a writers' book or magazine or publisher's guidelines may have left last week, so before you send the letter off phone the publisher's office and ask if the person is still with the line (see p. 10).

Your query letter should be no more than two single-spaced pages. Indicate the line the book is aimed for if it's a category publisher. Give the word count. Then, in a few paragraphs, try to hook the editor into wanting to read your manuscript.

Study the back-of-book blurbs of that line. Try to convey the flavour of your manuscript and the salient points of your novel – the characters, the source of tension and the resolution. Do not leave the editor in the air about the ending. Your own voice should shine through as it will in the manuscript.

Briefly detail any writing experience you have, and any special knowledge that is pertinent to the plot of your manuscript. For example, if you have had short stories or articles published, say so, and if your heroine is a vet you might add that you have had considerable experience as a veterinary nurse. Make sure that your letter is grammatically correct and professional.

If you have not already finished writing your book, complete it while you await a reply, which could take from a week to several months. Your book should be ready to post off *the minute you get a nibble from an editor.*

If the editor likes your query she may ask for:

♥ a synopsis or outline; or

♥ a proposal (the first three chapters with a synopsis); or

♥ the whole ms (although this is increasingly rare).

The terms *synopsis* and *outline* are often used interchangeably, but generally a synopsis is a short summary of the story, roughly from two to six pages single-spaced. Some editors now prefer a double-spaced synopsis. If in doubt check. Few editors will turn down a good query because of spacing, but if they express a preference go with it. More and more, editors are judging professionalism as well as talent, and expect authors to have done their homework.

An outline is more detailed and may be up to ten or – in the case of longer books – even twenty or thirty pages. An outline conforms more to the shape of the book, and a *chapter outline* is just that: a list of chapter numbers, with a brief summary of what happens in each one.

Send whatever the editor asks for.

There is no 'right' way to write a synopsis, but certain key elements must be included.

Unlike most romance novels, a synopsis is written in the *present tense.* If you use flashbacks and they need to be included in the synopsis, slip into past tense here.

A synopsis is told in *narrative form* without dialogue. (Though you may use short quotes to illustrate or enliven the narrative.)

The synopsis should tell the editor:

♥ what sort of person the heroine is;

♥ what sort of person the hero is;

♥ what the source of tension or conflict is that keeps them apart for 200+ pages;

♥ what happens to bring the tension to breaking point, i.e. what events trigger the climax of the story; and

♥ how the tension is ultimately resolved.

One way to begin is to express the essence of the story in a clear, pithy sentence:

♥ Melinda was raped as a teenager, but when she marries Slade she tries to keep it secret from her husband.

♥ Slade returns from jail and discovers Melinda has a child everyone assumes is his – but he refuses to accept paternity.

♥ Melinda married Slade to gain her inheritance, but he wants to make the temporary arrangement permanent – and real!

This is called 'starting with the hook' (sometimes called premise). It states the source of the tension in clear, one-dimensional terms and is an excellent way to grab an editor's attention. Editors like to have a clear, easily grasped 'hook' to present to their marketing departments to help advertise and sell the book.

If you have an intriguing first scene in mind you may like to start with that. Or plunge into it immediately after stating the hook or premise.

You can try writing a 'blurb' of the book (like the ones that appear on back covers), and then fill out the story from there.

Or you may start with strong character sketches of the hero and heroine, especially if the tension between them hinges on the fact that they are very different personalities with diverging life goals.

A character sketch is not a physical description. In a synopsis, describing the character's appearance is unnecessary unless it has direct bearing on the story. If the heroine is very beautiful and believes that the hero is only interested in her looks, or if the hero is lame or scarred and convinced a woman can only be interested in his money, this rates a mention.

But the essence of character is in personality and background, not appearance. This is what you want to think about and describe. The editor will want to know if Melinda's beauty and people's reactions to it have made her ultra-confident or perhaps cynical, or why the damaged hero should be so convinced that all women are gold-diggers.

For this reason you may need to include some of the characters' back story – what happened to them before their love story begins. Was poor Slade ditched by his fiancée after he was maimed? Have the men the heroine thought she might love been uninterested in her ideas while panting after her body?

Tell the editor *why* your characters behave as they do. Concentrate on the emotional turning points of the story rather than external plot events – the editor wants to know that you understand the importance of emotion; don't expect her to take that for granted.

The climax – the dramatic moment after which the lovers believe that there is no hope for them – should be introduced in the synopsis. And the resolution, where everything turns out right after all, must be there too. *Never hold back information from the editor.* Your stunning plot twist may be what spurs her to ask to see the ms. Coyness about your ending will only irritate her, or make her think you have written yourself into a corner and don't know how to get out of it. And she will *not* steal your wonderful plot and give it to someone else! If she tried, any other writer would be mightily insulted by the suggestion that she isn't capable of thinking up plots of her own.

Make your 'selling' synopsis pacy – you want the editor to read every word and be dying to read the ms. (NB a couple of New York editors suggest that if you send chapters with the synopsis, place the synopsis *after* the chapters.) Use lots of verbs, and don't clutter it with adjectives or redundant phrases. Don't try to be funny unless the book is funny. Let it *convey the flavour of your writing* and of the book you are trying to sell. Spend time on it.

Remember that a synopsis is a summary of the *entire* book, even when you are sending chapters along. Don't start where the chapters leave off. Begin at the beginning and go on to the end.

A synopsis is a flexible instrument. Many writers depart from it before they finish the book. You need not check every small variation or be afraid to take a new direction because the editor liked the synopsis. If it's still a good book, and essentially not a different book, they won't insist you stick to the synopsis.

Most important are your two *main characters* and their *motivations*. Do not include in your synopsis every minor plot point or all the secondary characters. Describing every scene will clog it so the editor has difficulty following the main thrust of the story. Be clear in your own mind *what* the story is about, *who* are the main characters, *why* they can't follow their inclinations although they are falling madly in love, and *how* they ultimately resolve their problems.

The setting (where) and the time-frame (when) can be included if they are important to the story. If you are writing a historical romance the period becomes important and you will mention that. If the story begins five years after Slade and Melinda had a sizzling affair you will want to include this information. But who, what, why and how are the main questions an editor wants answered. If you have answered them adequately and written a wonderful synopsis she will be on the phone asking to see the rest!

Unless otherwise requested, if a publisher asks you to send a proposal they want a synopsis and the first three chapters.

Do not make a career of writing three chapters and a synopsis. Always get on with that or the next project after you've sent off the query.

Markets – finding a publisher

Markets change all the time. Publishers create new lines and cancel others. New publishers start up, established ones are taken over or change their requirements. So we have not attempted an up-to-date list.

Publishers usually list their address on the title page or back of the title page in their books. Study recently released books and see who published the kind you want to write.

We can tell you that Harlequin is the largest publisher of romance in the world, and at the time of writing the Torstar Corporation owns Harlequin Enterprises in Canada, Silhouette Books in New York and Mills & Boon in London, all of whom publish series or category romances. They have distribution operations in other countries, and their books are translated into more than twenty languages.

Other publishers have smaller romance lists, in named 'lines' and in single titles.

Several books published annually list publishers and their requirements. These include:

♥ *Writers' & Artists' Yearbook* (A & C Black, UK) – gives a breakdown of publishers by fiction genre, including romantic and historical.
♥ *The Writer's Handbook* (Macmillan, UK) – lists romance.
♥ *Writer's Marketplace* (Boatsman, Australia)

♥ *The Novel and Short Story Writer's Market* (Writer's Digest Books, USA) – lists romance and historical fiction together.

Writers' magazines often give market information. Some are the journals of writers' or romance writers' societies. Many of these addresses will change, and magazines and writers' groups come and go. Try your library or local writers' group for up-to-date information.

♥ *Heartstalk*: Romance Writers of Australia newsletter; P.O. Box 1363, Cleveland, Queensland 4163, Australia.
♥ *Heart to Heart*: Romance Writers of New Zealand newsletter; P.O. Box 80–204, Green Bay, Auckland, New Zealand.
♥ *Romantic Times*: 55 Bergen St, Brooklyn, NY 11201, USA.
♥ *Romance Writers' Report*: Romance Writers of America magazine; 3707 FM 1960 West, Suite 555, Houston, Texas 77014, USA.
♥ *The Romantic Novelists' Association News*: Romantic Novelists' Association magazine; address changes with changes of executive officer – see current edition of *Writers' & Artists' Yearbook* for up-to-date address.
♥ *Writer's Digest*, Writer's Digest Books, 1507 Dana Avenue, Cincinnati, OH 45207, USA
♥ *Writers News*, PO Box 4, Nairn IV12 4HU, UK
♥ *Writers' Guide*, 11 Shirley Street, Hove, East Sussex BN3 3WJ, UK

On the Internet you will find romance readers' and writers' chat groups and email loops, and publishers' and writers' sites. These too are fluid and can change. Go to a search engine and look for subjects like romance, romance readers, writers, romance writers, writing groups, romance novels, and writers and writing.

In many countries there are romance writers' organisations. These groups run conferences, organise workshops, and will offer support and assistance. Current addresses may be found in the writers' books and magazines above, but if you have trouble finding them write to us care of A & C Black for addresses.

Or visit http://www.voyager.co.nz/~dclair and email us from there.

10. Occupation – Writer: being professional

A professional attitude is the mark of the real writer. Some people want to be writers; some people just want to write. Real writers write. They also:

♥ Find out what sells – not twenty years ago, but now. Some romance publishers will send guidelines to help writers who provide a large, sufficiently stamped addressed envelope (or envelope and International Reply Coupons if overseas).

♥ Read a lot – and widely – and because they need to know what's happening in their field they read lots of recent romances.

♥ Analyse the books they read – and also their own work – very carefully, in order to isolate whatever it is that they like from the books and endeavour to reproduce it without copying another author's style or plagiarising her work.

♥ Subscribe to writers' and readers' magazines and groups where they will learn what readers and publishers want and what changes are taking place in publishing houses. Many of them are finding internet email groups extremely useful for up-to-the-minute news and information.

Invest in your writing, even if at first you're not earning much – most jobs have a training period before you begin to earn a living. Writing is no different. There are many good books about writing, about setting out your work, about the publishing business. You will need to buy good paper, envelopes and stamps, and have some kind of filing system.

Manual typewriters are inadequate tools for today's writers. If you do use one, clean the keys and change the ribbon before typing your final clean copy.

Buy a computer or word processor with a good printer as soon as you can, and learn how to use them.

You don't need the latest and greatest with jangling bells and piercing whistles, but you should buy what you can afford – perhaps an outdated secondhand machine which you can pick up quite cheaply.

Inkjet printers are cheap and adequate. Laser printers have dropped in price and will stand up better to being asked to print two hundred or four hundred pages continuously.

A good typing chair is a must if you are going to spend long hours working. You need to look after your back. Take exercise – sitting all day is bad for your health.

Once you get started

Set up a timetable and write regularly. Professional writers do – otherwise they'd starve.

It can be difficult if you're not earning money from your writing yet, especially if you have family commitments, but you are never going to earn money if you don't start keeping professional hours of some sort now – which may only be an hour or less a day, or one day a week, but should be faithfully adhered to.

Aim to work for half an hour if you can't spend any more time, or to write at least a page. At a page a day, even without working weekends, you will produce 260 pages in a year, more than is needed for a short category romance.

Research

Research, because someone out there will know if your facts are wrong. Romance readers are astute, intelligent, articulate women; we have received letters from corporate managers and consultants, Nasa scientists, university academics, women in the professions, businesswomen, and women working in the home. All of them enjoy reading romantic novels – and if they can't trust you to get your facts right, they may well decide not to read you ever again.

Research when and what you need to – and only as much as you need to. Research is a splendid way of procrastinating while maintaining the illusion that you are working at your writing. As many writers have discovered, the Internet is an invaluable research tool – or a great time-waster.

Join writers' organisations and online writers' and readers' email groups; read writing magazines; haunt the how-to-write section of your local library; buy books like this one or at least get them from your library, and good general reference books; go to conferences; take courses if you think they'll help.

Use your imagination

It is not professional to use someone else's plot with all the incidents and plot devices changed a little – however old the romance is.

That said, there are basic and classic situations that readers still like (see pp. 43–5). A fresh, new approach to the Cinderella plot, for example, is going to excite both editors and readers.

Don't put in the funny thing that happened to your neighbour last week, or cast your hated sister-in-law as the villainess – you can use real incidents to build on, but if you use them unchanged you run the risk of not being true to the characters in your book. A novel is a highly artificial production; real life has a habit of looking completely out of place in it.

Don't use generic characters – the stereotypical arrogant hero, the slinky, sophisticated Other Woman, the demure heroine. Even the feisty heroine. Think about your characters; give them pasts and personalities and motivation so that they leap off the page.

Mechanics

Know your grammar rules – if only so that when you break them you know exactly why you're doing it.

Check your spelling, and don't trust your computer to know the difference between 'their' and 'there' or 'two' and 'too'.

When you write for a publisher across the Atlantic, they will probably not expect you to conform to their spelling. They will change it in the copy-edits or leave it as is. Let them tell you if they expect you to change things.

Keep up-to-date

Write about characters that are true to their generation. Your readers have kept up with the times, and so have the editors you hope will buy your books. Some of them will be younger than you.

If you only read old secondhand books your writing will reflect this. A manuscript takes up to two years from acceptance to publication, so if you add another year – or several – when you buy the books secondhand, you're out of tune with what's currently wanted by the editors. And what readers are reading now.

Editing and rewriting (you're not finished yet!)

After you've completed your first draft:

♥ Go through it for typos (typing mistakes) and spelling and grammar mistakes, or other infelicities (see checklist overleaf);

♥ If you have a literate friend or relative whose objectivity and knowledge of English you can count on, ask them to check it again, but –

♥ Under no circumstances allow anyone who doesn't read and enjoy romances to critique it. If your friend is not a romance reader, tell them you want *only* spelling and grammar checked. No comment on the story. Don't hand it around for other people to criticise.

♥ If you have not already done so, send a query letter (see pp. 84–9) to an editor of your choice. If an editor has already seen a letter, synopsis or proposal and has expressed interest in seeing your work, it is no longer an unsolicited ms, and you should address it to that editor, marked 'requested material'.

Checklist for editing and rewriting

♥ Typos and spelling errors. If in doubt look them up.

♥ Uninviting passages – paragraphs all the same length, too dense, or consisting of sentences of all the same length. Long chunks of narrative or introspection unbroken by dialogue. Or pages of dialogue without accompanying action or body language.

♥ Confusing/amusing passages due to sloppy grammar, inadequate punctuation, poor sentence structure.

♥ Redundant words and phrases – she thought *to herself*; he shouted *angrily*; *she saw that* he was; the house was *situated at*; *there was*; etc.

♥ Over-reliance on adverbs and adjectives, rather than verbs – *He walked unevenly* (use *he limped*).

♥ Clichés and vague word usage – *sparkling eyes, muscular chest, twinkling stars, attractive figure, tastefully furnished.*

♥ Unintentional ambiguities and Freudian slips, double meanings, *especially* in love scenes! (*laid, screw, stiff, prick*, etc.).

♥ Unintentional repetitions of words and phrases, especially if they are unusual.

♥ Inconsistencies: blue eyes in one scene, green eyes in another. Also in settings (the design of houses, etc.), or characters' speech patterns.

♥ Over-explaining – telling the reader what's happening instead of painting the scene and letting the reader pick up the inferences.

♥ Melodramatic language describing the emotion, instead of its cause or its effect – *her heart was wrung with pain, his heart sang with joy*.

♥ Over-reaction – irrational anger or overwhelming erotic fervour without sufficient cause/motivation having been established or implied by the author.

♥ Extraneous frills, e.g. descriptions of places, things, events that are not integrated into the story, add nothing to the mood or the reader's knowledge of the characters or plot, and do not *emotionally involve the protagonists*.

♥ Dialogue that is stilted and unrealistic; or is too realistic, includes boring greetings, introductions, etc. and uninteresting speech patterns; or does not *advance the story or add to knowledge of the characters*.

♥ Disguised repetition – saying the same thing in two different ways within a sentence or paragraph (*'Yes, thank you, sir,' he said politely*). Repeating the same dilemma over and over in every chapter. Having the characters re-enact an argument several times. Describing a relationship or situation in narrative and then having it acted out in a scene. Seeing the scene and then having a character describe it either in dialogue or internal monologue. The golden rule is: 'I will say this only once!'

Assessment

It is not professional to write to a published author and ask her to look at your manuscript. She's busy writing her own books, and she might be working on a manuscript that bears a resemblance to yours in some way – in which case she'll probably feel it necessary to rewrite hers, because she knows that even a hint of a whiff of a suggestion of plagiarism has ruined careers.

In the end a publisher's opinion is the only one that matters.

If you can afford it, you may want to send the ms first to a professional freelance editor or book doctor (one who is a romance reader and editor, not someone who despises the genre and knows nothing about it). A freelance works for the writer, not the publisher, and her job is to point out any flaws in the ms to the writer so that the ms is as clear, well-written and free from errors and typos as it can be before it goes to a publisher. A good editor will check on plotting, characterisation, motivation – all the things we have mentioned in this book – as well as spelling and grammar.

At this point a critique – where the editor reads the manuscript and writes a report on its strengths and weaknesses – might be more useful than a full edit with corrections. We both use a freelance editor, which saves us a lot of time.

If you can't afford that, and don't have a literate and analytical friend or relative whom you trust, who loves romance and might do it free, put the ms away and start on the next book. Work on it for at least two months; then go back and re-read your first manuscript.

Probably you will see great holes in the plot and the characterisation; actions and dialogue which appear to have no motivation; and sentences which go on forever and don't make sense.

Correct these, then print out a fair copy.

Never send off your only good copy – manuscripts have been lost in the post. If you use a typewriter, photocopy the entire manuscript. Then send the photocopy or printout to your chosen publisher. Do not send a computer disk or electronic submission unless the publisher requests it either specifically or in their guidelines.

Presentation and layout of your ms

The professional writer always submits to her editor a manuscript that is clearly presented in standard manuscript format. The following guidelines will ensure that your manuscript will not strain your editor's eyes, and will show her that you have taken the time to find out how to present a manuscript properly.

Paper: good quality white A4, 70–80 gsm copier paper is accepted world-wide although US standard is shorter.

Font: if you have a choice, use 12pt Courier font because it is the easiest to read, or something close to it. Some writers use 12pt Times Roman. Fancy script or sans-serif is unsuitable.

Setting out: use one side of the paper only, fully double-spaced lines, margins 3cm (1.5 inch) all round. Keep the same number of lines (25–27) per page, except for chapter ends and beginnings. Indent each paragraph five spaces (unless a specific publisher indicates otherwise). Insert extra spaces between paragraphs only when you wish to indicate a time lapse. Don't justify (i.e. even up) the right-hand margin even though computers do it beautifully. It makes it hard for the publisher and printer to calculate length. Note: not all professional typists know how to set out a manuscript.

Corrections: keep them minimal. Use correction fluid and a fine black pen for very minor corrections. Retype or reprint if the page looks messy.

Italics: underline any words you want to come out in the book as italics. Do not use your printer's italic print – publishers don't like it. A single word such as 'I' could be missed by the publisher's printer when it is italicised in some fonts, whereas an underlined word always stands out.

Page numbers: follow consecutively from the previous chapter – don't start at page one for each new chapter. Most publishers prefer numbers in the top right-hand corner. Each page should carry an identifying keyword from the title and/or the writer's last name (e.g. 'Writer/Dream/100'). Write your pen-name here if you're using one.

It's okay for a sentence to carry across two pages. If the last page of a chapter consists of one line, move it to the previous page if you wish.

Misnumbered pages: at the end of the page, print in square brackets '[page # follows]:' and at the top of the next page print '[follows page #]' – e.g. page 48 follows page 46, or page 47a follows page 47. Square brackets normally indicate matter that is not intended to be printed.

Chapters: start each chapter on a new page, a third to halfway down. Type the chapter number (usually in words, e.g. Chapter Two). Leave three more double spaces and begin the first paragraph. An average chapter contains approximately twenty to thirty typed pages, although this may vary widely, especially in longer books. From ten to thirty pages per chapter is reasonable for a short book. Most publishers have no set requirements.

Word count: make sure you know how many words the publisher you're aiming for wants. No matter how wonderfully you write, their budget does not allow them to print books beyond a certain size, especially in category romance where the printed books all have the same number of pages. But some computer word counts don't count white spaces; what the publisher is really buying is x number of pages. You can use the computer's character count and divide by 5, or manually count up about 8 representative pages and divide by 8 to get an average. Once you know what the format you have set-up on your word processor gives you, you can quickly count up your words in future books.

A rough guide based on 12 point pica type: 26 lines per page = approximately 250 words; 20 pages = 5,000; 100 pages = 25,000; 200 pages = 50,000; 220 pages = 55,000; 240 pages = 60,000; 280 pages = 70,000; 300 pages = 75,000; 320 pages = 80,000; 340 pages = 85,000; 360 pages = 90,000; 400 pages = 100,000; 600 pages = 150,000; 800 pages = 200,000 words.

Title page: centre the title about halfway down, and two spaces below type the author's name as you wish it to appear in print. State the number of words to the nearest 500 (for books). In one corner of the page place your name and address, and if you wish you can add, 'Copyright Jane Writer' and the year, although this is not strictly necessary. Professional publishers know your work is copyright from the moment you have written it. Another way is to put a discreet copyright notice at the end of the ms.

Last page: your name and address should also appear on the last page, below the word 'END' or the symbol ###.

Packaging your ms: Do not fasten or bind pages with staples, paper clips or fancy binders. Use large rubber bands or slide the ms into a strong plastic bag of snug fit and/or place in a box, or wrap well to withstand posting. Bubble bags are fine if the ms is rubber-banded or tightly wrapped first. Minimum wrapping means minimum postage, but you want your ms to withstand post office handling.

Always keep a clean copy with every alteration in it. Send the original or a good photocopy. If you're submitting a photocopy, note on the title page 'Not A Multiple Submission' (if this is true) – see below.

Contacting editors

Unfortunately, competition in the romance field is so fierce, and the editors so overwhelmed with manuscripts from hopeful writers, that many ask for a query letter or query and synopsis before they will even look at chapters or a full ms. So the ability to write a great query letter or synopsis has become an important part of the professional writer's armoury (see Chapter Nine, pp. 84–9).

Until recently sending the same work to different editors was regarded as unethical. Some still dislike it – look in writers' guides or contact the publisher to find out. You may decide to take the risk of a multiple submission anyway, but it is probably not wise to send the same ms simultaneously to different lines or branches of the same publisher. Sometimes an editor will pass on to a colleague a ms she feels is not for her line but might fit elsewhere within the house or group.

Choose a publisher which prints the kind of work you are offering. Write to publishers asking for their catalogues, or ask bookshops and libraries for their used ones.

Read writers' magazines, publishers' trade magazines, writers' markets books, and the book pages in newspapers and journals. And find an editor's name, and address the ms to her/him. Use contacts. Or phone the office and ask for a name. Some houses won't accept a manuscript without an editor's name, and if the editor has left, the ms will be returned to you unread. So check.

Postage

If you want the manuscript back in the event of rejection, enclose a suitable stamped self-addressed envelope. You can also enclose a stamped self-addressed postcard and request it be posted to acknowledge receipt by the publisher.

If you are sending a manuscript overseas enclose a letter-size self-addressed airmail envelope and one or two P.O. International Reply Coupons, and in your cover letter indicate that the publisher need not return the ms.

A returned ms is usually unfit to be sent to another publisher anyway; better to write off the cost of making another copy against the expense of postage. And if it has been rejected you're probably going to redraft it before you send it away to another publisher.

Records

Note the title, where you sent it, and the date. If there's no reply in 2 months (3–4 months if overseas) politely enquire with an SAE and Reply Coupon if the editor has had time to consider it. If there's no reply 3–4 weeks after that write again, pointing out that you have had no response to your ms and letter (giving dates of posting). After 2–4 weeks send another good copy elsewhere. Keep dated copies of all correspondence and have a filing system so you can always lay your hands on a letter. You might keep everything about one book in a file or box, perhaps · along with a copy of the ms and/or a disk of the final copy, or file everything from one publisher in one place.

Daphne keeps an inward/outward mail book, with information on when and where she sent letters or manuscripts, received replies from editors, and any other relevant business mail – bills paid, subs sent, etc. – so she always knows when something arrived or was sent.

Acceptance

When you are accepted by a romance publisher they will prefer that you write regularly for them, and you will be assigned an editor to work with.

Your editor may ask you to make alterations, and if you refuse the publisher will know that you're not professional in attitude, and they won't be very keen on publishing any future book of yours. They're in it for the long haul; they want a writer they can work with.

Change everything that won't violate your conscience or your integrity as a writer. If you feel very strongly about something discuss it courteously and be prepared to listen and to compromise. Both you and the editor are after the best book you can produce.

Any relationship you forge with your editor will be professional. Oh, it can be friendly and supportive, but if you send your editor a bad book she's not going to publish it, even if you are in the habit of sending funny birthday cards to each other.

Rejection

If the publisher says they don't think this manuscript is worth publishing, and that they don't feel you should do any more work on it, they won't expect to see it back again. And they'll know if you just change the names.

But you won't do that – after all, by the time you get the editor's letter back you've almost finished the next book.

And if they say that your source of tension is not strong enough they'll expect you to come up with a much stronger one in this book.

Because that's what being professional is – learning from your mistakes, doing the very best that you can, and striving always to do even better than the last time.

Agents

At the time of writing category publishers are very open to unagented manuscripts, although this may change. An agent may not be able to do very much for a category author in the way of negotiating better contract terms. But some category writers do prefer an agent to talk to their publisher about money matters and find the (usual) 15% commission worth it.

If you write a bigger book it may be difficult to sell without the help of an agent. Both Britain and America have agents' organisations that accept only reputable agents into their ranks and insist they maintain professional standards. Many of these agents are in the British and American writers' market books we have listed for you.

These organisations frown upon agents who charge reading fees.

If an agent recommends a particular freelance editor or book doctor, check with a writing group or knowledgeable person before employing either the agent or the book doctor.

Publicity

Writers are now expected to be publicity conscious. Some actively court the media, send newsletters to fans and friends, pay for advertisements, bookmarks, postcards and giveaways to publicise their latest book, maintain home pages on the Internet – or hire a publicist.

No one knows if personal publicity helps to sell books. If it isn't your style simply say no. But if you say yes remember:

It isn't professional to slag the romance genre – *or any other genre* – to journalists, or to run down other writers. If directly asked for an opinion on an author, book or genre you dislike, say something like, 'She/he/it brings a great deal of pleasure to a great many people.'

Try not to discuss other people's work. It is easy to be misquoted, especially if the journalist has a hidden agenda. Make your comments as positive as you can and keep them short and clear so they are less prone to manipulative editing. And always remember, nothing is off the record, even if the cameras aren't running and the microphone is turned off.

The Payoff

Publishers pay by the royalty system. You, the writer, receive a certain percentage of the cover price of every book sold.

Writers are usually advised not to accept a one-off flat payment for a book.

The royalty percentage varies; on hardback books the rate is generally around 10%. But most romances appear in paperback.

Paperback royalties range from 2%–8%, the higher rates normally given to well-known writers. Most publishing houses have rigid contract clauses about royalty rates, and you may not be able to negotiate a higher rate until you have proved yourself not only a big seller, but a consistent producer of books.

Writers' organisations consider any rate below 5% to be too low, but there are honest and extremely efficient publishing houses who pay below this. Because they have excellent distribution systems they sell a lot of books, and their writers don't complain – overmuch.

Legitimate publishers nearly always pay an advance on royalties. This too is negotiable, but often not for new writers. The more important you are on your publisher's list, the higher your advance and the more advantageous the terms. Some publishers pay in steps – perhaps a third on signing a contract, another third on acceptance of a finished or revised ms, and the final third when the book is published, which is usually at least a year after the ms is accepted. There are many variations on this pattern.

This advance is just that – an advance. Before your book delivers any more money to you it has to earn out that initial payment. Some never do. Make sure your contract specifies that in that event the advance is non-returnable.

Royalty statements are made up twice a year, but they don't cover the immediately preceding six months. Thus the statements you receive at the end of May will be the amount your books earned in the period June–December the previous year.

Royalty statements are bywords for what appears to be deliberate obfuscation, but they are slowly becoming easier to read and understand.

How much each book earns depends entirely on how many people buy it. Writing is not a career for people who need the security of a steady pay cheque!

11. Ethics and Morality

Copyright

Copyright exists from the moment a writer commits her words to paper. A copyright notice simply affirms that the writer knows this. It is not strictly necessary to put a copyright notice on your manuscript, and although many writers never send off a ms without one, some editors prefer not to see it on the title page; if you wish to pander to their little quirk you can place a discreet one on the last page. The form is: either the international symbol 'c' in a circle (©) or the word 'Copyright': followed by the date and your name. Even if using a pseudonym it is best to have the copyright in your legal name.

When the book is published the publisher will include a copyright notice in your name or pseudonym.

NB: Writers use pen names for a variety of reasons which usually have nothing to do with being embarrassed at what they are writing, but if you don't wish to there is no need. Do understand that if you become very, very popular you may have to take measures to ensure your privacy.

Plagiarism

Plagiarism is the worst sin a writer can commit, the equivalent of a bank manager embezzling funds. Anyone proven to have filched another writer's work will find her career is over, and even an unproven charge may wreck a writer's life and livelihood. *This has happened.*

So never use another writer's words, and never, never, *never* allege someone has stolen your work unless you have incontrovertible proof. Mud is a very sticky substance and it is unforgivable to accuse a fellow writer on mere suspicion.

Writers store in their subconscious everything they see, hear and experience, so a phrase or name seen elsewhere may surface unsuspected in your work. Some phrases and expressions have become common currency. But you may not deliberately reproduce a striking image or sentence from someone else's work, whether published or unpublished.

You cannot lift passages word for word, or use them slightly altered. Although ideas, titles and plots are not copyright, you should not knowingly copy plot ideas or incidents from other writers, unless to use them as a springboard for a new and original twist on an old tale. Striking similarities between the characters and plot development of two books by different authors have been the basis of lawsuits.

There are probably no totally new plots, especially in popular fiction, and there are obviously many similarities within any genre. Ideas often occur to more than one person at a time. Edison in the US and Swan in England each invented an incandescent light bulb at roughly the same time. We once independently each presented the same original, clever, never-before-used title to a publisher at the same time, and a third writer narrowly pipped us both to the post.

Sometimes a new writer is convinced that someone has stolen her idea, plot or characters, but unless the words are identical it is highly unlikely, and it would be unwise and unprofessional to suggest chicanery to anyone, no matter what you might suspect. You could lay yourself open to a charge of slander or libel. Accidental similarities occur in literature all the time.

However, keep copies of everything and record every submission. If you do need to prove your words have been used without permission, you will have the necessary evidence.

'Morality'

Sometimes romance writers are censured for the sexual content of their books. Critics have assumed that the readers of romance are either very young or are unable to form sound judgements on their reading.

The average reader is a woman of over thirty-five. We do not write for children, but if you don't wish to write about overt sex, there are publishers and lines catering for readers who prefer not to read about it. Some publishers also have 'young adult' lines for the teen market.

Write what you would like to read and what seems right to you. A story has its own momentum and its own integrity which demands your attention and respect.

Stories in which the couple have no more physical contact than a chaste kiss on the last page, in which no single word has a sexual meaning, can simmer deliciously with underlying romantic tension.

If the story *needs* a love scene, that's what you write, with as much detail as seems appropriate. You can decide later if you want it published in its original form or not. But do not write as though your elderly mother, your minister or your children are peering over your shoulder. Censorship has no place in a first draft.

Romance is based on sexual attraction, and leaving the sexual element entirely out of a love story is like leaving the apple out of an apple pie. But how much cinnamon and spice you flavour it with is a matter of personal taste.

Unless you deliberately violate your own beliefs, your deeply felt moral and ethical standards will come through subtly in your writing, even if the characters are not always living up to them. Your characters may do something that shocks you, but this is not you. You do not need to wrench them out of their skins and force them into better behaviour.

Allow your characters to weather the consequences of their actions without authorial intrusion. Trust your reader to work out for herself that the characters' mistakes and imperfections only compounded their problems, while sincerity, honour and integrity helped to resolve them.

Immoral earnings

Romance is sometimes sneered at by those who know no better. For a long time it was regarded as beneath the notice of any serious writer or reader because it is a women's genre and anything only women did was automatically not as good as what only men did. Even fellow scribes take sideswipes at romance writers, some suggesting it is a heinous crime to make money from writing instead of starving in a garrett.

We have letters from readers telling us our books have cheered them out of depression, given them hope when they saw none, helped them solve problems in their relationships, made them forget pain and illness and grief for a little while.

While we write not to teach but to entertain, our books affirm the value of life and love and commitment to the future. These are important human concerns recognised as such by our readers. We are proud to be writing for them.

Academia and Feminism

Academic and feminist tomes have been written about the dangers of presenting women with fantasies of ideal men and relationships, encouraging unrealistic expectations – or conversely of depicting brutal men with patriarchal attitudes, encouraging women to accept their supposedly downtrodden lot.

Both these bafflingly contradictory views presuppose that although male readers are not encouraged by their reading of thrillers and westerns to crawl along the top of an express train and shoot somebody, female readers are incapable of recognising the difference between fantasy and reality. Furthermore, it supposes they are not actually entitled to any fantasy – and who needs fantasies more than women?

Appendix
Fiction Techniques: Tricks of the Trade

You will see many good books whose writers have ignored some established literary practices, but the following general principles will be useful when you are writing or rewriting. These techniques are not rules – the only unbreakable rule is Rule Number One: There are no rules.

The hook

Start your novel with characters in a scene where something is happening, not with landscape, flashback or character description. Here are some ways of doing this:

Casual continuation

> When Melinda got off the plane in Rotorua, Slade Hunter was standing at the barrier, conspicuous because of his height and his air of controlled power. As she walked by him to the terminal, his hard grey stare followed her.

(Jumping into the story as though the reader already knows Melinda. The reader will trust the writer to give her more information as she needs it.)

Dramatic effect

> When Melinda Deere arrived at the office building, Slade Hunter was standing at the top of the steps – the executioner waiting on the scaffold with axe in hand.

(Introducing both protagonists in the first sentence while hinting at tension or conflict between them.)

Conversational

'Slade Hunter's here,' Melinda's secretary told her as soon as Melinda walked into the office that Monday morning. 'He's been waiting for twenty minutes and I think he's going to start chewing the carpet any second.'

(Dialogue attracts the eye, luring the reader in, just as most of us can't help listening in to conversations in public places.)

Describe the heroine

subtly, without her looking in a mirror. Not *Melinda Deere had red-gold hair which contrasted with her pale face.* This is straight reportage which jerks the reader out of the story and into a newspaper article. Try:

'Slade Hunter's coming *here?*' With a hand that shook slightly, Melinda Deere pushed a lock of red-gold hair back from her pale face.

(However, don't clog your writing with too much of this. Filter it in. If you've described the heroine fully by the end of the first chapter, that's fine. And you don't need to keep referring to her red-gold hair and large green eyes on every second page.)

Introduce the hero as soon as possible

Describe him as the heroine sees him. You are revealing the effect he has on her.

Not:

He had a cleft chin.

Try:

Melinda had always had a weakness for cleft chins.

Or:

Melinda's forefinger itched to trace out the cleft in that square chin.

Don't tell – show

Not:

> She was angry.

Try:

> Her red-gold curls seemed to crackle with anger.

(Caution: don't fall in love with your wonderful image. Too many crackling curls will irritate the reader.)

Use strong verbs

He *strode* across the room, rather than he *moved* across the room. But don't do it so much that it makes for jerky, breathless reading – she *raced, hopped, crawled, jumped, skipped, paced*, etc. all on the same page.

Choose the active voice

rather than the passive:

Active

> A gust of wind bent the tops of the trees and flipped the hat from Jas's head. (from *Summer Seduction*, Daphne Clair)

Passive

> The tops of the trees were bent and Jas's hat was flipped from his head by a gust of wind.

(In the first excerpt the wind is an active force; in the second, Jas's hat and the tops of the trees are being passively acted upon. The verbs *bent* and *flipped* are strong and immediate. Using 'was' dampens down the vigour and energy of the action and of the sentence.)

Moving in time

Indirect

Chapter ends, or double-line spacing between paragraphs; often combined with –

Direct

A week later, she woke in her hotel in...
Some time afterwards...
It was spring when...

Repetition

...agreed to go on a picnic on Saturday.

(double space)

Saturday it rained.

'...and dinner will be at seven.'

(double space)

At exactly seven Melinda entered the dining room.

Getting there from here

Use double spacing and omit journeys

'We'll go to see Mother,' Melinda said. 'I'll book the ferry tomorrow.'

(double space)

'You didn't need to come all this way,' said her mother.

Or straight narrative

The crossing was accomplished in an hour, and twenty minutes later they were sitting in her mother's lounge.
'I'm going to marry your daughter,' Slade said. 'Any objections?'

Omit uninteresting arrivals and departures

...she opened the door to Slade. Five minutes later she was pouring coffee when he came to lean on the kitchen doorway. 'I'm going to marry your mother,' he said. 'Any objections?'

(double space)

After he left, she cleaned up the spilt coffee and hoped he hadn't realised that she'd wanted to throw it at his head.

Dialogue tags

Make most speeches short. Break them up with actions and/or interruptions from others. Avoid long-winded characters.

♥ Use 'said' rather than awkward replacements (intoned, opined, riposted, etc.):

'Go to hell,' he said indifferently.

♥ Use adverbs (how something was said) only when the tone is not implied in the dialogue:

'Because I love you!' he told her furiously.

♥ Or use action cues instead:

'No, I don't love you.' He replaced the cup with a clatter. Melinda took a deep breath. 'I think you do.'
'I'm sorry, I don't.' Slade stood up and walked across to the window. 'I'm going to marry your sister.'

Description

♥ Landscape needs people and movement. There should be a viewpoint character emotionally involved in the scene, and if you describe a beach, have a fisherman casting his line into the water, or someone walking a dog along the sand. If you want an empty place with no people, use active verbs to give the picture life.

Trees whipped about in the wind. The waves foamed and tumbled to the shore.

♥ Inanimate objects should usually be given to someone to use – anything more than a cursory description should not be static. If you want to describe something that can't be handled, say a picture on the wall, it should have some emotional effect on the person viewing it.

The slashing black lines and dark, confused background made Melinda uneasy.

♥ People should be shown in motion, and their clothes while being worn.

Broad-shouldered in a well-cut shirt, and with legs that seemed to stretch for miles, he strode through the press of people... (*Tiger, Tiger*, Robyn Donald)

Even if the character is unconscious you can liven up the description with action.

Another wave came in, soaking the legs of his trousers and eddying about the woman's body, lifting her hair so that it streamed out towards the shore, revealing a blue swelling around a gash on her temple that must have bled for a while before she died. (*Carpenter's Mermaid*, Daphne Clair)

(Note the words that describe movement – came in, soaking, eddying, lifting, streamed, revealing, bled. Even 'died' is a verb.)

Information

Feed information in gradually, not in large chunks. Tell the reader just what she needs to know in order to see the scene and understand the emotions. In the first few pages, and even further on in the book, hold something back to tease her along and keep her turning those pages.

Characters shouldn't 'tell' each other what they both already know, but may well fire it at each other in shock or anger.

'You can't marry my sister – she's still at school!'
'So were you when we met – and you told me you were twenty-two!'

Flashbacks

First ask: is this journey back in time really necessary? If it is –

♥ Use double spaces and/or word cues:

...but it was years ago, that summer in Rotorua.

(double space)

Summer was the children's favourite time...

♥ You may need to use 'had' once or twice to inform the reader where the narrative is going.

On her sixth birthday Melinda and Slade had promised to marry each other. They were at the beach and had just built a sandcastle. 'This is the castle we'll live in,' he said, poking a flag into the top turret.

♥ Signal the return journey:

(double space at end of the flashback)

That was back when summers had been always blue and shining...

or:

(double space after flashback)

And now Slade was saying he wanted to marry her mother!

Be specific

Not:

...a blue dress

but:

...a skimpy satin dress the electric blue of a summer sky

Not:

> ...the seafood looked delicious

but:

> ...fat, luscious oysters glistened in their hard, frilled shells, and huge prawns curled in a pink heap on a bed of ice.

Omit rather than alter
Often if you are looking for a replacement word you will find it's better to cut it out altogether (especially adverbs and adjectives). Other words often best omitted: Yes, no, well, very, quite, suddenly.

Use the telling detail
The hiss of bubbles breaking at the edge of a wave, the glint of sunlight on a diamond ring, the slight flutter of a skirt in the wind creates an image without going into lengthy description.

Avoid
♥ Wordy constructions:

Not:

> The house which was situated at the top of the cliff...

But

> The house perched on the cliff...

♥ Redundancies:

> placed under arrest, advance notice, last of all, two twins, usual custom, unproven allegation.

Bibliography

Bright, Laurey; *The Rainbow Way*; Silhouette Books, 1987.

Buzan, Tony; *Use Your Head*; BBC Publications, 1989; with Barry Buzan; *The Mind Map Book*; BBC Publications, 1993.

Campbell, Joseph; *The Hero With a Thousand Faces*; Princeton University Press, 1949.

Campbell, Joseph; *The Power of Myth*; Doubleday, 1988.

Clair, Daphne; Harlequin Mills & Boon: *Grounds for Marriage*, 1996; *Reckless Engagement*, 1997; *Summer Seduction*, 1998; *Take Hold of Tomorrow*, 1984; *The Wayward Bride*, 1989. New Concepts Press: *Carpenter's Maid*, 1997.

Donald, Robyn; Harlequin Mills & Boon: *The Colour of Midnight*, 1994; *Dark Fire*, 1994; *A Forbidden Desire*, 1998; *A Matter of Will*, 1989; *Tiger, Tiger*, 1997.

Dunnett, Dorothy: Lymond series, Cassell; Niccolo series, Michael Joseph.

Frye, Northrop; *The Secular Scripture*; Harvard University Press, 1976.

Gabaldon, Diana; *Outlander* (*Cross Stitch* in UK); Dell, 1992

Krentz, Jayne Ann; *Dangerous Men and Adventurous Women*; University of Pennsylvania Press, 1992.

Mann, Dr Peter; *A New Survey – The Facts About Romantic Fiction*; Mills & Boon, 1974.

Mitchell, Margaret; *Gone With the Wind*, 1936.

Nabokov, Vladimir Vladimirovich; *Lolita*, 1955.

Thurston, Carol; *The Romance Revolution: Erotic Novels for Women and the Quest for a New Sexual Identity*; Urbana: University of Illinois Press, 1987.

Index